Dement[ia]
and the family

Rachel Johnstone

This book helps you to help your loved one to stay active, involved and engaged. You will surprise yourself just how much of the person you love is still there - waiting for you to find them.

Paul Smith, CEO, Dementia.REP

For more activities and information about dementia please visit:
www.parentsandfamilies.com

Acknowledgements

Dr Paul Smith PhD,
Advanced Nurse Practitioner;
CEO, Dementia.REP

Loraine Butterworth,
Admiral Nurse Clinical Lead,
Cornwall Care

Saul Mason,
Admiral Nurse,
Cornwall Care

Shiobhan Pickering,
Community Matron for Dementia

Carol Sprake,
Caron Cares

Jayne Vale,
Dementia Specialist and National Dementia
Care Award Winner, Helping Hands

Margaret Lovell,
Carer and Admiral Nurse

Heather Penwarden,
Founding Chair, Honiton Memory Café,
Devon Federation of Women's Institutes

Angela Thompson,
Co-ordinator, Sid Valley Memory Café

Text © Rachel Johnstone

Dementia and the family © Southgate Publishers.Ltd

First published 2014 by Southgate Publishers Ltd, The Square,
Sandford, Crediton, Devon EX17 4LW

Design and illustrations by Daniel Loveday
www.daniellovedaycreativesolutions.com

Printed and bound in Great Britain by
Latimer Trend, Plymouth

British Library Cataloguing in Publication Data.

A CIP catalogue for this book is available from the British Library.

ISBN 9-781857-411782

www.southgatepublishers.co.uk
www.parentsandfamilies.com

Dementia and the family

56 years old and grandfather to 23 children (including three great-grandchildren), Norman McNamara was diagnosed with dementia six years ago. He has done an enormous amount to educate others about dementia and he is the most powerful, positive and passionate champion of dementia awareness.

When I was diagnosed with dementia in 2008, there was virtually no help out there for someone my age and, because of that, I also found out what a lack of understanding about dementia there also was, and so our 'quest' began.

As soon as I met Rachel Johnstone I knew we would get along famously as we both had the same drive to change things, and the energy and passion to do what we believed in. I knew I had found a 'Kindred Spirit'. We became friends over the years and so when I was asked to write a foreword for her book, I was delighted.

I think the most important message to come out of this book is the message to children. *Dementia and the family* is about involving children and helping them to understand that dementia is a disease of the brain, and not something you just get when you are older. If that was the case, we would all have dementia when we age, it's as simple as that! But, to quote a well-known phrase, 'children are our future' and it will be the children who take this very important message forward; therefore, reducing the terrible stigma that is, at the moment, attached to dementia.

My own grandchildren bring me so much laughter and pride – and a diagnosis of dementia doesn't change this. Being a grandfather is an important part of who I am. This book reaffirms the role that children play in bringing a sense of normality and fun to the family – and this is all the more significant when dementia is diagnosed.

This book is written in what I call the good old-fashioned way, full of common sense; it's clear, concise and to the point, without all the confusing technical jargon that is so apparent these days. The activities are simple to do, and some may seem like just everyday tasks; but to those with dementia, they may offer a whole new experience, or help bring back memories of what they used to do – it is so important to remember these treasured memories.

Since my diagnosis, our quest to raise awareness has allowed us to speak at many conferences, create a global Dementia Awareness Day, or DAD day as we like to call it, and even have lunch with the Prime Minister at 10 Downing Street. None of this could have been done without the help of my own angel, my wife Elaine.

So, thank you Rachel Johnstone for all you do, and will do in the future.

Norrms McNamara and family

This book has one aim: to enable you, as a family, to live well with dementia.

All too often, a diagnosis of dementia can pull the family apart, leaving caring relatives feeling utterly powerless to help, and worrying about the impact of a change in a loved one's behaviour on younger members of the family. This needn't be the case. Talking to children and young people about dementia in an open and honest way, involving them in caring, taking steps to make the home dementia-friendly, discussing new ways to communicate with your loved one and taking part in meaningful, intergenerational activities can bring the family closer together.

In particular, the treasure trove of activities in this book will create opportunities to spend quality time as a family, build new memories, reduce the stigma surrounding dementia and give you confidence and self-belief in the difference you can make to the life of your loved one with dementia.

This book is built on three important premises:

1. Dementia cannot (yet) be cured or reversed but it can be managed. Whilst you will not be able to change the medical diagnosis or prognosis, there is something you need to know: you can greatly influence the quality of life and well-being of your loved one with dementia. There are indeed things you can do, so you needn't feel powerless.

2. You must focus on the person (your loved one) not on the illness or the signs and symptoms of dementia, when it comes to caring for them. A person with dementia is just that: a person with dementia, defined by their interests, previous occupations, quirky ways, passions, personality and everything else which makes them the person you know and love.

3. The role of the family is crucial in dementia care. It isn't just our own individuality that makes us who we are; it's also our relationships with others that define us and give us our intrinsic sense of self-worth. In particular, relationships with grandchildren provide feelings of pride, emotional fulfillment and reinforce your loved one's role and standing within the family unit. It is also within the family that memories are preserved and where memories take on extra meaning because those close to you relate to, and treasure, your unique recollections. It is these shared stories that reinforce our own sense of identity and personal and family heritage.

This book is all about offering an assortment of dementia-friendly, family-focused activities. However, first of all, you need to ensure that children understand dementia, how it is likely to affect their loved one and how, in time, they might need to adapt some of the ways in which they communicate. The first section lays the foundation to enable the whole family to benefit from the activities by appreciating what it means to live well with dementia and considering some of the changes you may need to make. The guidance in this first section also encourages you to step back as a family, reflect and 'take action' by completing various tasks, activities and discussion points.

In the first section of the book, you will also find some information on why doing different activities is so beneficial to someone living with dementia and in order to maintain and strengthen family relationships. You will be guided through the 'preparation stage' before you undertake the activities and you'll be given tips on how they can be used.

Alongside this book, we have created a website: www.parentsandfamilies.com. The website includes further activity ideas and links to other websites, books, resources and organisations you may find useful. Additionally, it includes a number of frameworks, templates and checklists for you to 'Download and do'.

There are 160 different activities in this book – and many more if you take into consideration the adaptations and alternatives. Given that the starting point for deciding on the appropriateness of an activity is your loved one's interests and preferences, there is a diverse range, catering for all tastes and abilities. Many of the activities include some suggestions on how they might be simplified for someone in the later stages of dementia, and you will find further guidance on how to adapt activities on the website. It's up to you to choose which activities to try out first and we have included a downloadable record sheet on our website so you can make a note of how well the activity was received. You will also find a framework to help you design your own dementia-friendly activities at the end of this book.

What makes these activities special and dementia-friendly? Well, they are all based on some underpinning principles that spark off memories and stimulate engagement in a person with dementia: social interaction, music and movement, reminiscence, tactile stimulation and use of props, repetition and use of the 'muscle memory', a sense of achievement and usefulness, and an intergenerational approach. The activities have also been designed in such a way that there can be no feeling of 'failure'. It is about ensuring that your loved one is appropriately stimulated, without being over-challenged, as this can lead to frustration, anger and despondency. Worse still, being over-challenged may confirm their secret fears of being incapable and worthless when this is really not the case. It's just that their capabilities have shifted.

Who is this book for? Our aim is to help families to live well with dementia, and there is a range of activities to suit children and young people of all ages, interacting alongside their loved one with dementia. However, this is a versatile publication and activity workers within care homes, coordinators of memory cafés, enablers and care workers, and people working within day services and voluntary organisations will all benefit from using this book, substituting the notion of the family with that of the 'group'. As well as being used within the family home – and in the case of some activities, out and about – the activities can be delivered in care homes. Sometimes families can find it difficult to engage with their loved one, meaning that visits might become awkward and less frequent. The activities within this book, which could equally be instigated by a care worker, could help to bridge that gap.

Caring for, *and about,* a loved one with dementia

It is often the little things that make the biggest difference. Knowing how best to care for someone with dementia can be overwhelming – but you don't have to become an 'expert' in dementia care to improve the quality of life for your loved one. The little gestures, small acts of kindness, considerate behaviours and words of comfort – things that are all too often overlooked in our busy lives – are the foundation for caring for, and about, someone with dementia.

Ten ways to show you care

1. Savour every moment that you spend together by giving your undivided attention. Be there, and be totally present in the moment.

2. Treat your loved one as the person you know and love by being genuine in what you say, your body language and your eye contact. Treat them with respect and avoid being patronising.

3. Always acknowledge their feelings – even if you may disagree – and allow the person to release their emotions.

4. Wherever possible, involve your loved one in decisions. Never force them to do anything they don't want to do.

5. Involve them in conversations and don't exclude them or talk over them as if they are not there.

6. Find ways to make life a little easier, without taking over. Help to compensate for the effects of their illness whilst supporting their independence.

7. Look for every opportunity to engage in some creative activities and play games, share jokes, laugh, reminisce about funny stories and acknowledge your loved one's sense of humour. Activities and hobbies that your loved one has always enjoyed are particularly important since they help to retain their sense of identity.

8. Find ways to stimulate all the senses – from taste to touch – such as going for a walk and listening to the birds sing.

9. Try to be understanding and see things from your loved one's point of view. Never blame someone with dementia for their actions – or criticise or ridicule.

10. Keep to the rhythm of their life, being respectful of daily routines. Do not put pressure on your loved one to 'keep up', such as talking too quickly.

 **Discuss together.** Talk through these ten small, but significant, ways to make a difference. What effect would the opposite action have on your loved one? For example, how would they feel (and what would happen) if you didn't give your undivided attention and were always distracted by something else when you were with them?

 Download and do. Visit www.parentsandfamilies.com for a discussion tool to help family members understand the positive and negative consequences of their everyday interactions and behaviours.

It is important to understand that even though your loved one's memory, knowledge and language may be impaired, they still retain their own 'uniqueness' as a human being. It is not difficult to see the signs of well-being – the difference you are making – if you are getting things right. This will include gestures of affection, initiating social contact and evidence of self-respect (such as a pride in appearance).

 Download and do. Visit www.parentsandfamilies.com for a framework to help you record the signs of well-being and ill-being. Are there any other signs that indicate the contentedness of your loved one that you would add to the list?

Being surrounded by family and people who know you when diagnosed with dementia makes all the difference. Whilst the memory of someone you love may be fading, your family helps to 'hold it in place' by retelling stories from childhood, recreating magical moments from years gone by, revisiting favourite places, and partaking in activities, games and hobbies that you have always known and loved. That is one of the reasons why doing activities as a family unit is so central to well-being – to stimulate memories, focus on remaining strengths and abilities and to retain that all-important sense of self.

 Discuss together. It is crucial that all the family – especially the younger members – understand the reasons behind taking part in activities together. It's not just about the fun and enjoyment – there are therapeutic and psychological benefits as well.

It is natural for adults to want to protect children from anything that may upset them, but it is best to be open and honest about a diagnosis of dementia in the family. Every child will understand, and deal with, their loved one's dementia in a slightly different way and this is largely influenced by both their developmental and chronological age. One thing that is true of children of all ages is that they will respond to the emotional reactions of adults in their life. If you take a positive approach to dealing with your loved one's dementia, then so will they. Here are some practical tips to help you tackle the difficult discussions about dementia:

- Children can only usually absorb a little information at a time. Talk about dementia – and tell them what you know – in a gentle, calm manner, allowing the child to ask questions or express their worries.

- Make sure you 'pick your moment' when your child appears ready to talk – and there aren't any distractions that may take their attention away from what you have to say.

- Avoid euphemisms and use direct language, where possible. Dementia isn't easy to understand, so make your explanations as straightforward as you can.

- Checking to see if a child has understood what has been said is critical. Ask questions to check their understanding. There is nothing wrong with saying that you don't know the answer, and then getting back to them when you have had a chance to consult with a professional or a trusted source of information.

- Sharing your own feelings with your child can help to normalise what they might be feeling themselves. Sometimes children may appear unaffected by what is going on around them – but this does not mean that they are oblivious.

- Children tend to attribute physical symptoms to emotional experiences, more than adults do. For example, how often have you heard of your child complain of a tummy ache before a school test? This is a physical symptom of a worry they may have, and it is something you need to be aware of.

- Younger children may express their feelings of worry or concern through play, instead of verbalising how they feel. Older children are likely to want to know more about the facts regarding dementia.

- Throughout the illness, a child should be told about changes in their loved one's condition as they arise. If you can, you should allow your child to care for their loved one in a way that he or she chooses.

 Discuss together. It is very important to ask your child what they know about a loved one's illness. This enables you to find out about any misconceptions they may have. It will also help you to know where to start from when it comes to talking to your child about dementia.

Memory is a very complex, interrelated and fragile function of the brain. Whilst it is beyond the scope of this practical guide to provide detailed, scientific explanations of how our multiple memory systems work, there are four 'burning questions' relating to memory that it is useful to understand:

1. *Why does a person with dementia often remember all kinds of details from their past, but struggle to recall things that happened very recently?* The part of the brain responsible for storing new memories is called the hippocampus. Dementia strikes the hippocampus first. Long-term memory is said to be more resistant to the diseases that cause dementia, as long-term memory is stored, and embedded, throughout the brain in different regions. When dementia does begin to spread to other regions of the brain, it is the memories from the most recent past that are lost first. That explains why some people with dementia may recognise photos of their adult children when they were younger, but not photos from more recent years.

2. *Why does a person with dementia often repeat himself or herself, or ask the same question over and over again?* The hippocampus plays an important role in 'indexing' memories and sending them out to the relevant parts of the brain for long-term storage. If the hippocampus becomes damaged by dementia then it becomes incapable of registering and storing a new 'event'. New information quite literally goes in one ear and out the other! A person with dementia will repeat themselves because the brain doesn't register that the question has already been asked. You can't teach your loved one not to repeat themselves because, again, this is new information, which can not be taken in or stored by the damaged hippocampus part of the brain.

3. *Why does a person with dementia not remember who someone is, yet still shows signs of affection towards them?* Factual memory is stored by the hippocampus and emotional, feelings-based memory is stored by the amygdala. As described above, the hippocampus is the first part to be affected by dementia, so it follows that factual memory goes first and emotional memories remain intact for longer. Consequently, although a person with dementia may not remember who someone is, they will get a 'sense of feeling' towards them. Someone with dementia is also much more aware of the emotions and moods of others, and has a heightened sensitivity to picking up on moods and feelings. Therefore, if you are in a happy light-hearted mood, this is likely to be replicated by your loved one.

4. *Why is it that a person with dementia can recall intricate details of years gone by (and even remember what has just occurred) one day, yet struggle the next day?* The brain is known as a 'plastic organ'; it is very malleable and adaptive, even when it is damaged. Your loved one's memories, and some of their abilities, are affected by the way various areas of the brain communicate with each other at any given moment. Emotion, music, smells, sounds (and more) can help to stimulate damaged, but often accessible, areas of your loved one's

brain. The message is this: never stop trying and you will be surprised at just how much of the person you love is still there, waiting for you to find them.

Discuss together. It is difficult for children to grasp how it feels to have dementia. It can be helpful to come up with scenarios, or stories, that children will be able to relate to. For example, use the following anecdote to explain about factual memory and feelings-based memory. 'Imagine that you are going away on an activity week. You feel excited, nervous about meeting new people and slightly stressed about everything you have to pack. Now imagine feeling that range of emotions, but not being able to put your finger on the reason why. You have completely forgotten the factual reason behind your feelings. You cannot remember where you are going, what you need to pack and who you are going with. How would you feel?' Your child might identify feelings of panic, anxiety, confusion and disorientation. This mirrors what someone with dementia would feel, and examples like this will help to improve your child's understanding and empathy.

Download and do. There are plenty of websites that explain more about how the brain and memory works. This could be something that you research together as a family. For a useful video that explains how the brain is affected by dementia, see www.parentsandfamilies.com.

Explaining dementia

The changes that come with dementia are hard enough for adults to handle. In order for children to accept the changes in their loved one, they first need to understand a little more about dementia. Although it may be distressing to talk about dementia in such a frank and honest way, children and young people may actually be relieved that their loved one's behaviour is down to an illness and not because the person with dementia doesn't love them any more. The pointers below will help you to explain what dementia is. You can choose whichever ones you feel would be most appropriate and make sure you adapt your explanations to fit the age and understanding of your child.

- Dementia is caused by many different illnesses, which damage the brain cells.

- When the brain cells become damaged, they cannot grow again.

- Our brain controls everything our body does – from recalling our memories to keeping our heart beating. If we experience damage to the brain cells and structures in the parts of the brain that control our basic life functions, then our body will start to shut down.

- There are more than 100 known causes of dementia. The most common type of dementia is Alzheimer's Disease, which according to the Alzheimer's Association accounts for around 60–80 per cent of cases of dementia.

- Dementia is a progressive illness, which means that the brain becomes increasingly damaged over time. This also means that the symptoms of dementia get worse. In the early stages of illness, you will notice only very minor changes in your loved one's capabilities, behaviour and capacity to remember. As the illness reaches the late stage, your loved one may fail to recognise those closest to them, and they could become restless and distressed. They may also become very frail and lose control of their bodily functions.

- There is no medical cure for dementia.

- Dementia is not contagious.

- Dementia isn't just a natural part of getting old. One in three people over 65 will die with dementia, according to the Alzheimer's Society.

- Every day is different for a person with dementia. There can be good days and bad days.

- Someone with dementia can become very muddled and confused. They may do things like putting the newspaper in the fridge (instead of the milk), dressing with their clothes back-to-front, forgetting what day of the week it is, living in the past and being convinced that they are of school-age, thinking that a younger relationship is actually their spouse or parent.

- Common symptoms of Alzheimer's Disease and other forms of dementia include memory loss (especially for recent events), difficulties with tasks that require organisation and planning, problems with speech and language, changes in personality and mood, difficulty performing familiar tasks, and depression. However, you have to remember that no two people will have symptoms that develop in exactly the same way. Furthermore, some other forms of dementia have specific symptoms, such as visual hallucinations.

- While people with dementia will lose their ability to remember, their capacity to experience and feel as human beings is largely unaffected.

- Dementia is extremely frustrating for the person who has been diagnosed – especially in the early stages when they are aware of the impact it has on their life and those around them. However, as a family, you can make the biggest difference to their quality of life.

Discuss together. Metaphors can help explain things in a way children can relate to. The way we lose our memory can be likened to an onion. It is the recent memories that peel away first, like the outer layers of an onion. Norrms McNamara describes the effects of dementia as like a Christmas tree, where the lights go out one by one, starting with the light that helps you to remember recent events. However, you can shake the tree to switch the lights back on again. Doing the activities in this book, as a family, is a metaphorical way of 'shaking the tree' of someone with dementia.

 **Download and do.** By understanding how someone's memory is affected by dementia, knowing more about the illness and considering the many ways to show you care, it is easy to see that there are lots of ways the family can help. Visit www.parentsandfamilies.com for a 'checklist template' to identify the steps you can take as a family to support your loved one with dementia.

Creating a dementia-friendly home

At both your family home, and the home of your loved one, there are some simple, small changes you can implement that will make a big difference. As the disease progresses, your loved one may find it harder to move around, struggle to remember where they put things, forget where the toilet is and not recognise familiar objects. Making some of the changes outlined below will create a comfortable, safe environment for you all to enjoy each other's company, avoiding confusion and encouraging familiarity.

- Do a quick safety walk round your house and see what might become a trip hazard, or a trigger point.

- It will help if the colours of walls, floors and doors are different to help the person with dementia to get their bearings.

- If possible, avoid large patterned flooring or wallpaper, as this can confuse the eye and even cause people to hallucinate.

- Use contrasting colours for the crockery and cutlery, placemats and chairs so that they all are easily distinguishable.

- Pick a toilet seat in a contrasting colour – and ideally the flush – to help draw attention to it and distinguish it from the rest of the bathroom.

- Keep the bathroom door open so that it can be found easily.

- Fit glass doors to cupboards, or simply remove cupboard doors. If food can be seen, the person with dementia is more likely to remember to eat.

- Purchase an old-fashioned kettle and toaster as these will stimulate recognition from childhood days and will be more 'familiar'. Fitting taps of a traditional design will also aid recognition.

- Ensure that lighting is adequate. By the time people reach 75, they need nearly four times as much light as a 20 year-old to see properly.

- Ensure any mirrors are easily removed – as sometimes someone with dementia can struggle to recognise their own reflection.

- It will help to label drawers, by using large text, images and colours.

- Put up a big clock, displaying the day and date.

- Use personal photographs, ornaments and special paintings to trigger memories and make the room feel homely. In the later stages of dementia, it may be more beneficial to use old photographs, rather than recent ones of the family.

- Provide a range of stimulating activities around the home, such as puzzle books, jigsaw puzzles and picture books.

- A fish tank can be relaxing and therapeutic to watch. Looking after a houseplant can also be beneficial.

- Ask for advice from your local occupational therapist or social services department, if you feel you need it. They may also be able to help you explore telecare options, such as personal alarms, automatic lighting and calendar clocks. In negotiation with your loved one, put up tasteful signage around the house that draws attention to essential things such as the toilet, the bathroom and keys, for example.

Discuss together. Of the changes listed above, what could you do as a family? Involving children will help to make the situation, and adjustments around the home, more normal for them. For example, you could design some labels for drawers, cupboards and rooms – using text, colour and images. Please note that we are not advocating that you change everything all at once in either your home or your loved one's. Such a drastic change would be unsettling and confusing. Instead, make a couple of adjustments and see how these help your loved one to orientate themselves around the home.

It is a good idea to ask children to design the signage you use around the house, especially as they may include a picture. A person living with dementia may lose the ability to read printed words, so having a picture as an extra aide-memoire is an ideal dignified solution.

Conversation is caring: communicating with your loved one

Given that each person with dementia is unique, everyone will experience their own individual difficulties with communicating. Your loved one might have trouble finding a word, get sentences jumbled up, fail to understand what you are saying or interrupt or ignore you.

The key to caring conversations is to take time to think about how it might feel to have dementia. This will help you all to come up with strategies to help your loved one cope, retain their dignity, communicate their likes and dislikes and enjoy the art of good conversation. Communication is fundamentally important because without it, we lose our sense of identity and self-worth as an individual person.

Communication isn't just about what you say:

- 55 per cent is in our body language, facial expressions, posture and gestures
- 38 per cent is the tone and pitch of our voice
- 7 per cent is the words we use.

Body language is a particularly powerful means of communication for a person with dementia, and especially for those with language impairment. In fact, even if your loved one is no longer capable of communicating verbally, they are often still capable of communicating non-verbally.

As the disease progresses, communication skills can deteriorate, and children need to be prepared for this. It is better to stick to one-to-one conversations, allow more time for the person to respond, and break down tasks with very clear step-by-step instructions.

 Above all else, it's ok if you don't know what to say. Just being there will help. This is arguably the most important point about communication to share with your child.

The following tips are aimed at helping your child to communicate with their loved one.

Starting out

Firstly, you may have to speak more slowly, using shorter sentences, and only talking about one thing at a time. It can be confusing if you introduce too many ideas or topics of conversation at once. This is particularly pertinent when introducing and explaining the activities contained in this book. Children need to be aware that their loved one's attention may wander, and not to take this personally.

It will help to call your loved one by their name (or grandad, grandma, etc) as this will not only anchor and orientate them, but it will attract their attention (and for the child, it reinforces their relationship with their loved one). It can also be beneficial to refer to the location of where you are, the day of the week or the time of day. Children need to be prepared to be mistaken for someone they are not, such as another relative.

Given that so much of the way in which we communicate is about our body language, children need to be aware that their loved one will pick up on their facial expressions, posture and their general enthusiasm for the task in hand! Just smiling and offering reassuring physical contact can make a world of difference. Tone of voice is also significant and if you do start losing your patience, this will be picked up in the tone of voice even if the words aren't understood! It can be helpful to use visual clues by pointing to objects, using props or creating flashcards.

Children need to know that their loved one may confuse the 'present-day reality'. They may revert back to their childhood days, as if they are actually there. If this is the case, then avoid correcting or contradicting them. It is far better to use your imagination and join them in their 'reality' – something that is far easier for children than adults! Remember that how someone feels – their engagement in the moment – is more important than being factually correct.

Discuss together. Your loved one's communication needs will change over time. You may find it helpful to write out the different ways in which you can aid communication on separate pieces of paper, or Post-It notes. Discuss with the family which communication strategies are likely to have the greatest impact and prioritise these using the 'Diamond 9' approach, explained at www.parentsandfamilies.com.

Listening well

Arguably, listening attentively is more important than speaking when it comes to effective communication. This is a crucial skill for all children to learn regardless of whether they have a loved one with dementia. It starts with ensuring that they give their full attention, and not letting their own mind wander. It's about savouring and genuinely appreciating the time spent together with their loved one. Children should understand the significance of showing that they are emotionally engaged in a conversation or activity by smiling, nodding their head or showing that they are listening intently. It will also help to reassure and engage the person with dementia if they try to match and mirror their body language and movements. Children should also try and read the emotions of their loved one. Sometimes the emotions being expressed are more important than the words being said.

Discuss together. It is a good idea to practise listening attentively through the use of role-play. As a parent, you could first play the role of someone who is not listening, so that children understand how this feels. This could be followed by a scenario where you demonstrate the signs of active listening, asking the child to identify the actions, gestures and techniques you used.

Children need to know that they should allow plenty of time for their loved one to answer and respond. They may need to gather their thoughts first and process what has been asked of them. It is important that your child is relaxed and avoids the temptation to hurry their loved one as this will only make them anxious.

Striking up a conversation

It is helpful to offer children guidance in opening up conversations with their loved one, and the advice outlined below should also be adhered to when carrying out the activities contained within this book.

Aim not to ask too many questions at once, so that the person with dementia does not feel pressurised or overwhelmed. Instead, you should consider beginning conversations with familiar phrases that your loved one likes to use, or which strike up happy memories from their childhood. This might be a well-known saying or a family 'in-joke'. What matters is that they immediately feel at ease and ready to engage. If your loved one has particular difficulties with verbal communication, then it will help if you also reduce how much you speak. That way, the communication between you becomes more genuine and two-way.

It is best to avoid questions linked to short-term memory – such as asking what they had for dinner – and those that require a factual answer. Instead, you should elicit responses that trigger feelings and opinions. Direct questions – such as 'what was the name of your first pet?' – can cause some distress as your loved one frantically searches in a missing vault of memories.

The best way to steer a conversation is to use sentence stems, such as:

- Perhaps we …
- I wonder how it was to …
- I've heard that …
- I wish I'd known what it was like to …

What to do if someone becomes upset

Sadly, anxiety is common in people living with dementia. As a family, you will need to discuss some strategies to support your loved one when they become agitated, upset or anxious. It is important to let your loved one be upset, if this is a release of emotions they need, but it's important to know when to intervene.

Here are some tips to guide the family:

- Find out what relaxes your loved one. This might be a hand massage, listening to music or a simple cup of tea in their favourite china cup.
- Do not argue: it will only make the situation worse.
- Remember that someone with dementia will pick up on 'signals' that demean or depersonalise them – and this includes non-verbal signals.
- If you find yourself becoming irritable, walk away (and do something that takes you away from the situation, such as going to find something upstairs). Your loved one will only pick up on your mood and this will cause further upset.
- Don't be afraid to admit to difficulties – but don't be disheartened.
- There is sometimes a case for deflection tactics. For example, if your loved one asks to see their father (who died years ago), you could divert the conversation by asking about the things they used to do with their father.

For your family, doing activities together provides a means to connect with the person you know and remember. When your world has been turned topsy-turvy by a diagnosis of dementia, activities bring you all back to quality time, together, as a family. For your loved one with dementia, activities help to improve self-esteem, express feelings, rediscover their sense of identity, build on their capabilities and, most importantly, bring a sense of pleasure and enjoyment to their day. They will also offer reassurance for your child and a sense that it is still possible to retain a relationship with their loved one.

What is more, research has shown that whilst your loved one may not remember doing a particular activity, they may retain the feelings they have experienced through doing that activity. The aim of an activity is simply to ensure that your loved one enjoys doing it – as the feelings of happiness you engender will stay with them. That is your measure of success – not whether the activity is completed or whether you hold their concentration for the duration.

The most successful activities are likely to be those that incorporate your loved one's interests and hobbies from the past. These will be associated with well-being and will 'make sense', triggering positive feelings and associations. Doing activities that you love makes you feel good about yourself. However, it is also worth bearing in mind that curiosity does not dissipate with dementia, so don't be afraid to try something new and see if it works.

By doing activities, you really can make a difference!

Be prepared

Before anything else, preparation is the key to ensuring that the activities you do together are effective, enjoyable and have a positive, lasting effect. In fact, 80 per cent of the effort is in the preparation and 20 per cent is in the actual delivery of the activity. Yes, really!

So, what do you need to do before you start an activity? Here is a list of bases you need to cover:

- Just as we all have our good and bad days, this is equally true for someone with dementia. Dementia affects people in different ways and no two days are the same. Don't be disheartened if, on a particular day, it doesn't work out.

- When picking your time to run an activity, minimise change to familiar routines and respect important routines in daily life.

- Remember that someone with dementia can lose their sense of time, such as by getting lunch and dinner times muddled up. As dementia progresses, your loved one's attention span and concentration will decrease, meaning that they will become easily distracted and have difficulty focusing.

- It is important that you always 'invite' your loved one to participate in activities, so that they still have a choice, and say, over what they do. Rather than asking an open-ended question – such as 'what activity would you like to do?' – it is better to provide a choice between two options.

- It is very important that the family always starts by explaining what activities they are going to do together and why. Don't just launch straight into an activity, as your loved one will be left feeling confused and anxious.

- As a family, make sure you are clear on how you are going to explain the activities to your loved one. If necessary, demonstrate things first – and find different ways to explain, other than words. You may need to think about breaking the activity down into different steps and explaining each step at a time. Use both verbal and visual instructions.

- People with dementia may lose the ability to initiate activities, so it is up to the family to get them started. For example, if you are doing a puzzle together, you may need to start off the puzzle yourself and then hand a couple of pieces to your loved one.

- When you have decided on the activities, be prepared with a 'Plan B' to make the activity less involved and complicated, if you need it.

- Before you begin, make sure the environment is as calm and clutter-free as you can make it. Minimise all distractions.

- Think about where you are going to do the activities, whether this is at a table or using a lap tray, for example. If you are visiting your loved one in a care home, is there somewhere quieter you can go?

- Be as creative as you possibly can in using props and recreating the 'moment of yesteryear'. For example, if you are organising an old-fashioned picnic, can you get hold of an authentic picnic basket of the time, dress in clothes of the time and eat the food your loved one would have eaten for a picnic of yesteryear? It is important to be as 'authentic' as possible.

- If you do need to offer to help, try and do things with, rather than for, the person.

How the activities can be used

An activity is defined as a 'specified pursuit in which an individual partakes'. It is anything that engages your loved one's attention, that they are actively involved in and that has a purpose. Activities can be structured or unstructured; they can last a day or just a few minutes; they can be leisure-based (such as completing a puzzle) or linked to everyday activities (such as folding napkins). Activities can also be stand-alone (such as a trip to the seaside) or incorporated into daily routine and tasks. For example, by finding ways for a person with dementia to contribute to tasks and chores, you provide them with a sense of having contributed to family life.

In choosing from the many activities that follow, you should pick those that match your loved one's existing strengths and capabilities to their interests. For example, if they particularly struggle with language, then pick those that rely on non-verbal communication or adapt other ones. Remember that what matters is the sense of enjoyment and accomplishment from taking part in the activities. It's about creating 'happy feelings', and even if your loved one may not remember doing a particular activity, feeling good but not knowing why is a quite different proposition from feeling bad and not knowing why.

Discuss together. As a family make a list of your loved one's favourite things and hobbies.

It is important that you take the activities and make them your own. They don't have to be prescriptive. It is hoped that you will be inspired to create your own – almost anything can be an activity. Look for opportunities to personalise the activity in ways that your loved one will relate to, resulting in a spark in their eyes. As dementia progresses, your loved one will rely much more on their implicit or procedural memory, which works on habits and the things you do instinctively.

Download and do. Hints and tips for creating your own activities and simplifying existing activities at www.parentsandfamilies.com.

As you carry out the activities, look for the signs that show your loved one is engaged and make a note of these. These visual clues may be something obvious, like smiling, or something a bit subtler, like stroking their ear. You are the best judge of whether an activity is 'working' or not. The chances are that if you are feeling bored and uninterested, then your loved one will be too. Don't forget that maintaining your own enthusiasm for the activity is equally important, since someone with dementia is much more feelings-based and will pick up on your lack of interest. Always remember the basic premise that if we fail, we disengage; if we succeed, we engage.

On the pages that follow, each of the activities offers a brief explanation for you to adapt, the props you need and a suggestion for how the activity could be adapted. Visit www.parentsandfamilies.com for even more activities.

1

A
1950s
Sunday

Description: Relive the 'good old days' as a family and trigger fond memories from the past. How much has your family life changed? A 1950s Sunday was a quiet day, centred around going to church, enjoying a Sunday lunch, reading the papers, relaxing in the armchair whilst listening to the radio and perhaps going for a gentle stroll. It also involved wearing your 'Sunday Best' – your best, and often most formal, clothes. Take a step back in time as a family and recreate the moment!

Props and Preparation: This activity relies on the simple pleasures: the Sunday papers, cooking a traditional Sunday lunch, the radio and of course selecting your 'Sunday Best' outfit.

Adaptation: Discuss with your loved one what they remember about their Sundays and incorporate these memories into the day. You could listen to popular lunchtime radio programmes of the past, such as the 'Billy Cotton Band Show' (which is available on the internet). You can adapt this activity for any other era, such as the 1960s or 1970s. This activity could be followed by a discussion on how family life has changed over the years.

2

Saturday
morning
pictures

Description: Combine a family outing to the cinema with an opportunity to reminisce about a trip to the 'flicks'. The Saturday morning pictures was the highlight of the week for many. A trip to the cinema didn't just involve watching a movie. There was a sing-song, vintage cartoons, talent shows and competitions, such as eating a donut on a string the fastest. Look out for screenings of old movies at your local cinema or stage your own Saturday morning pictures at home by watching old movies and vintage cartoons and taking a break for a choc ice. You could even come up with your own talent competition, such as seeing how many times you can bounce a ping-pong ball on a bat.

Props and Preparation: Keep an eye out for screenings of vintage movies at your local cinema, theatre or museum. If you are running this activity at home, then you will need to source some old movies and/or cartoons and buy in some choc ices.

Adaptation: Most cinemas had their own clubs, with their own badge and song that they sang at the beginning of each Saturday morning session. Does your loved one remember their cinema song? The ABC Minors was the first Saturday cinema club for children and it's possible to find the ABC Minors song and their badge on the internet.

3 — A trip to the seaside

Description: With some very simple additions, a trip to the seaside can be turned into a trip down memory lane. A traditional visit to the seaside involved setting up your deck chair, visiting the pier, eating sandwiches, going for a walk along the promenade, building a sandcastle, taking part in a rounders match, a donkey ride, sending a postcard about the wonderful day you had and enjoying fish and chips on the way home (whilst singing 'Ten Green Bottles'). How about that for a family day out?

Props and Preparation: Purchase an old-fashioned, wooden bucket and spade and some flags to go on top of your sandcastle to make your trip as authentic as possible.

Adaptation: Whilst at the beach, you could organise a stone-skimming competition, as well as one for the best sandcastle, of course! You might also like to collect shells and pebbles, which can be painted when you get home. If travelling to the seaside is too much, you could bring the entertainment to your loved one, in the form of a Punch and Judy show. There are showings that you can watch and record over the internet. You might also like to look at vintage seaside posters together, pass a beach ball around or suck on sticks of rock. Please visit www.parentsandfamilies.com for useful links.

4 — A ride on the steam trains

Description: A family outing on a steam train is one sure-fire way to create a multi-sensory experience for someone living with dementia. There is nothing quite like jumping aboard, hearing the chug of the engine and piercing shriek of the whistle, and smelling the combination of coal and steam and oil. As a family, taking a day out on a steam train is the perfect opportunity to take in the beautiful scenery and trigger fond memories from the past. An old-fashioned picnic will round the day off nicely.

Props and Preparation: You will need to book your trip in advance and it is worth checking out any access requirements. Make sure you leave enough time to visit the gift shop too, and pick up some items for reminiscence.

Adaptation: A ride on a steam train is the perfect opportunity to reminisce about travel and holidays. You may also wish to consider a visit to a museum specialising in travel and transport collections.

Using modern technology

Technology helps to bring memories to life – putting sights, sounds, video clips, audio recordings, music, photographs, news clippings and people's own individual memories right into your hands. Using technology to trigger conversations creates a truly shared experience between older and younger generations.

5

Watching old movies and television shows

Description: You can source a huge range of old movies and television shows from the internet, especially through YouTube. People with dementia lose the ability to follow a plot and one of the many great things about older movies is that they tend to have a simpler plot line.

Props and Preparation: Search for a selection of old movies and TV shows online. Whenever possible, it is important to offer choice at every given opportunity. However, keep it simple as someone with dementia can find too much choice confusing. Rather than asking an open question, such as 'what film would you like to watch today?', it is better to present a choice between two different movies.

Adaptation: If it's too much to hold your loved one's attention for the duration of a movie, then how about watching the adverts of yesteryear? With their catchy songs, these were often more memorable than the TV programmes! Another good alternative is nature documentaries. They tend to be visually stunning, without any complicated narration to follow.

6

Photos and slideshows

Description: Putting together a slideshow presentation of old family photographs, or images of the past, is a perfect project for children. You could select a theme, such as steam trains or 1950s ladies' fashion. It can be helpful to add a one-sentence description underneath the image, as a conversation starter, and you may also wish to set the slideshow to music.

Props and Preparation: It is important to take the time to find the right pictures. Each picture needs clarity so it immediately engages your loved one, without too much going on.

Adaptation: The photographs and images you use don't have to be related to your family life. In the latter stages of dementia, be prepared for your loved one not to recognise people or places in old family photographs. You could find generic, old photographs of things like knitted swimming costumes, school milk monitors or a mangle (an old-style laundry aid). You can leave a lasting imprint by curating your own personal story for your loved one using the site Historypin. There are full instructions at www.parentsandfamilies.com.

7 Discovering local history

Description: It's quite often the little details that trigger long-forgotten memories … a favourite meeting place during the courting years, a particular sweet shop run by an infamous local character. Historypin connects you to others who share these memories and who have created a record of them by adding their photographs and stories to the site. You can while away the hours by browsing Historypin – looking at old photographs and video footage and reading aloud people's recorded memories and stories. You can search by location (such as the town where your loved one grew up), by topic (such as street parties or tram travel) or even by a particular individual.

Props and Preparation: Visit www.historypin.com and see what information has already been shared about the local area. Create your own Historypin account.

Adaptation: Historypin enables you to share your own stories. Recording your loved one's memories – and showcasing them on the website – will help the person with dementia to feel valued and improve their sense of self-worth. You might also like to explore the possibilities of using Google Earth to remember earlier times in their life and 'see' the place they were born and landmarks that are familiar to them (www.earth.google.co.uk).

8 Advertising archives

Description: Kellogg's ran the world's first full-page advert in print in 1906 and, as a result, sales of cornflakes rose from 500 cases per day to over 2,900! There is a lot of history embedded within advertising over the years. Two websites, in particular, offer access to vintage adverts of yesteryear: www.advertisingarchives.co.uk and www.historyworld.co.uk. Visit these sites with your loved one and see what memories they spark. You might also like to create a slideshow of some of the adverts and you can access video footage of old television adverts via YouTube.

Props and Preparation: Visit the two websites and explore what is available to base a reminiscence session around the advertising archives. You might also like to prepare by researching old adverts on YouTube.

Adaptation: Set about creating your own advertising game. Print out large (A4-sized) versions of old adverts and on separate pieces of paper, type out the corresponding advertising slogan. The idea is to match the advert with the slogan.

9

Memory apps

Description: Whilst dementia makes it difficult for people to learn new things, advances in technology make it easier for people to enjoy creative activities and connect with the online world in ways that wouldn't have been possible before. Touchscreen devices, in particular, can play an important role in improving the quality of life for your loved one with dementia. You'll be amazed at what apps you can find – including memory aids, games, creative activities, interactive stories and even the opportunity to plant and nurture your own online garden!

Props and Preparation: With so many apps out there and so many possibilities for intergenerational activities based around technology, it can be hard to know where to start. Thankfully, there has been a lot of research on the best apps for people with dementia. Please see: www.parentsandfamilies.com.

Adaptation: As an alternative to touchscreen devices, try video games such as the Nintendo Wii. The games will not only be a huge source of family entertainment, but they will help your loved one's balance, coordination and mental stimulation. They can be enjoyed from the armchair and are suitable for all different abilities. The best games are the simple ones, such as the Wii Sports package that comes with the console. If your loved one likes to use a personal computer, then Internet Buttons is a free tool that allows you to create a simplified, personalised website 'front page' with direct links to all their favourite sites. See www.parentsandfamilies.com for more information.

Memory memorabilia

People with dementia can often remember the distant past more easily than recent events, and there is a lot that can be gained from capturing, triggering and sharing memories together. Not least, reminiscence activities will help your loved one to recapture their sense of self and feel valued for who they are now and how their past has shaped them. There are many ways to reminisce – including photobooks, writing down stories, making memory boxes and using technology.

Remember that reminiscence can also bring back painful memories or become upsetting for your loved one. Refer back to the section, 'What to do if someone becomes upset' for guidance, on page 17.

10 Memory Book

Description: Memory Books are a visual treasure-trove of memories and provide a special record of your loved one's personal history. There are no 'rules' about what to include, but you may wish to think about: family and special relationships, key life events, places your loved one has lived, likes and dislikes, favourite foods and recipes, hobbies and working life. You can use photographs and pictures, along with captions, or 'talking points', explaining the image. You might also like to add some tactile pieces to your page – such as ribbon, buttons or even a square of fabric from an old school tie.

Props and Preparation: It is a good idea to create a Memory Book together as soon as your loved one is diagnosed. It will not only become a very important, and comforting, memory aid – but it will be indispensable for everyone who comes into your loved one's life who doesn't know who they are as an individual person. You will need to decide whether you are going to use computer software to produce your own professionally printed book or whether you will use a home-made scrapbook. It is a good idea to find one where you are able to remove or add pages. See www.parentsandfamilies.com for a useful guide to creating Memory Books.

Adaptation: You might like to think about creating a book in the shape of a favourite pastime, such as a cricket ball. Rather than creating a record of a person's life story, you could theme your book. How about a Memory Book focused on their favourite sporting achievements and memories?

11 Scrap-booking

Description: Scrapbooking is a creative way to record and preserve the stories behind not only photographs, but also memorabilia, such as tickets, letters, newspaper clippings, postcards and more. The scrapbooking tradition has been around for a long time and your loved one is bound to recall their bright sugar paper scrapbook, filled with mementos from their time. In fact, a good way to start this activity would be to look up images of scrapbooks from years ago. This could very well trigger some long-forgotten memories and it will also help provide you with inspiration to create your own scrapbook, together. You may be fortunate enough to discover a box of mementos that your loved one has kept, such as a fantastic collection of old postcards, or you could start your scrapbook by finding pictures of old-fashioned bus tickets, adverts or postcards from the internet.

Preparation: Anything goes with a scrapbook! Almost as important as the end-product is the creative process of putting the items together, deciding on the layout and cutting, sticking and choosing the creative embellishments. This is a great way to involve your loved one in a meaningful activity. You will find some pointers on creating scrapbooks at www.parentsandfamilies.com. There has been a real resurgence in the popularity of creating scrapbooks in recent years, so your local craft store will have plenty of items you can use to create and decorate your book.

Adaptation: You may well find that your family gets a taste for scrapbooking – and children can be encouraged to create their own scrapbooks for holidays, school trips or around a theme, such as collecting memorabilia of their favourite football team. This introduces children to the concept of creating a 'time capsule', which others in the future will benefit from discovering and using – much like the way you are using old-fashioned items and photographs as memory triggers now.

12
Memory Board

Description: A Memory Board is another way to display important photos and images that mean something to your loved one. Think of it as a personalised picture, which you can hang on your wall, as a constant focus for reminiscence and remembering. You can either use a traditional noticeboard and pin up photos, images and mementos, or you can create a collage of memories behind a picture frame.

Props and Preparation: It is best if your Memory Board is at least A3-size, so that it can be easily seen from around the room. You can buy noticeboards with attractive frames or a picture frame that will fit in with the décor of your loved one's favourite room. You may need to scan the photos before you stick any pins in them or stick them down!

Adaptation: You can create more than one Memory Board to display around the room and use different themes. An alternative to Memory Boards is an Activity Board. For example, you can either create yourself, or buy, an Activity Board with a variety of different locks and latches securely attached to it. This will help to trigger memories about household tasks or DIY, as well as improving coordination and dexterity skills by undoing the locks and latches. For more information on Activity Boards, see www.parentsandfamilies.com.

13
Memory Box

Description: A Memory Box is a multi-sensory way to trigger memories from the past. Whereas Memory Books and Boards appeal to our visual sense, smell, taste and touch can be stimulated through the contents of a memory box. Smell, in particular, can bring back a flood of memories so you may wish to include a favourite perfume in your Memory Box. You could also add items like an old cricket ball, a trophy, an ornament, an item of clothing or some photographs. You can decide on anything you like – as long as it has meaning to your loved one. To bring back memories, the person with dementia should hold each item and be encouraged to share what that object brings to mind.

Props and Preparation: You can use anything you like for your box – from a decorated shoe box or old biscuit tin to a nice wooden box. However, you should try and use something that is hard-wearing. You may wish to label each item with a tag or create a list on a sheet of paper, with a brief summary of the significance of the item. As well as selecting items from your loved one's past, you could also think about the different themes you could use. For example, you could create a memory box on the theme of baking days and find old recipe books and kitchen implements from around the home and charity shops. If you like, you can even buy ready-made Memory Boxes online – but half the fun is in making your own!

Adaptation: Even if the person with dementia cannot participate verbally in reminiscing using items in their Memory Box, it can still give them pleasure to be involved in reflections on their past by holding and feeling the items. For someone whose dementia is in the late stages, it is important to make their Memory Box all the more multi-sensory. Think about all the different textures you can use and include things like ties, lace and buttons.

14
Lucky dip

Description: This activity is a variation on a theme of Memory Books, Boards and Boxes! Your loved one is bound to remember the traditional lucky dip, where an old bran tub was filled with sawdust and presents were hidden inside. Collect a range of reminiscence items – such as old-fashioned games, toys, books, etc – wrap them up and put them in a tub or sack. The aim of this activity is for your loved one to pick out an item, one at a time, and share their memories of that item.

Props and Preparation: This activity requires some preparation – in that you will need to collect the items, spend time wrapping them and source a suitable container. You may not be able to source an old bran tub, but a sack will do. Rather than using sawdust, you could obtain some small polystyrene shapes.

Adaptation: Unwrapping the presents is an additional, beneficial activity for your loved one, which can be incorporated into reminiscence. However, here is an alternative that works just as well (without the wrapping paper)! Ask a member of the family to select a reminiscence item from your growing collection, put it in a pillow case and tie up the top. You now have to pass the pillow case between you and guess what the item is inside by feeling it.

15
Sporting memories

Description: Old football programmes, photographs, newspaper articles, video clips, memorabilia and books can all be used to relive memorable sporting moments from years gone by. Perhaps your loved one has a favourite team and, together, you can compile a scrapbook of memories or a digital record of old footage and photographs? Are you aware of how much the 'beautiful game' has changed over the years? Ask your loved one about the days before branded football shirts, what it was like to head a heavy, old leather ball, the rule changes they have seen over the years and if they can remember when the £20 per week limit on players wages was abolished?

Props and Preparation: There are many places on the internet where you can find footage, photographs and memorabilia. Visit our website, www.parentsandfamilies.com, for some pointers. It may be possible to pick up a traditional, wooden supporters' rattle – which was used to cheer on your team, and was banned in the 1970s due to its potential use by hooligans!

Adaptation: Combining music with sporting recollections is another way to stimulate long-forgotten memories. How about singing old football songs from the terraces? You could also create your own sporting memories game by matching up the name of the club to the football strip (before the days of branded football shirts). Furthermore, you could play a game of Subbuteo – a tabletop version of football where you use your fingers to flick miniature figures of footballers. The possibilities for sporting reminiscence are endless – and remember it doesn't just have to be linked to football; you could theme your activities on the Olympics, for example.

Books and stories

The beauty of story-telling is that stories come from what you can imagine, not what you can remember. Story-telling will give your loved one an outlet for communication, when they struggle to express themselves through conversation. During a story-telling session everyone can contribute, everyone is equal and there are no rules. Did you know that we are best able to think, remember and learn in the late morning? Our alertness and ability to concentrate tends to slump after eating a meal, such as lunch. Be mindful of the timings of your story-telling sessions.

16
A picture leads to a thousand words

Description: Build your story-telling session around a photograph. Ideally, this should be a person with an evident sense of 'character' or a scene with people engaged in an activity. It works better if the photograph isn't of someone you know. Nominate one person in the family who can act as the story-telling 'facilitator', asking open-ended questions to guide the story. One person should write down the twists and turns of the story as it unfolds.

Props and Preparation: Choose an old-fashioned photograph and, if your loved one's dementia is in the moderate to late stages, pick one without too much going on as this can be confusing. Look out for opportunities to integrate songs into the story, and you may wish to act out different parts when recapping the story so far.

Adaptation: As a treasured memento for our loved one, how about turning your unique story into an illustrated picture book? This can be created on the computer or using a scrapbook. There are even websites where you can share your special stories for all to enjoy. See www.parentsandfamilies.com.

17
My life story

Description: Use your loved one's Memory Book – a record of their life history – as a basis to retell familiar stories from different times in their life. The aim of reading aloud their recorded memories isn't to prompt them to remember events and embed these in their minds, it is purely and simply about retelling their stories in order to trigger the feelings of happiness associated with them.

Props and Preparation: A Memory Book, or a Life Story Book, is a biographical record of your loved one's life. A Life Story Book made with the person will have more meaning and value for everyone involved, which is why the recording of your loved one's memories should be a priority even before a diagnosis.

Adaptation: Instead of writing stories down – and rereading them – you could decide to film your loved one telling their stories in their own words. There is a guide to using film to hear the voices of people with dementia on www.parentsandfamilies.com.

18 Scripted fantasies

Description: A scripted fantasy is a method of transporting your loved one to a different place in time by using a pre-prepared, highly descriptive 'script'. You ask them to sit with their eyes closed and visualise as vividly as they can a particular scene as you describe it. As the script-reader, it is your role to help them to see the scene in their minds, to smell the smells and hear the sounds. You should use short, very descriptive and detailed sentences, ensuring that your voice is slow and expressive, pausing to allow the listener to take in the scene they are imagining in their minds.

Props and Preparation: You first need to decide on a list of topics as the themes for your script. Pick one and spend some time researching it. For example, you could describe a picnic on a summer's day when your loved one was in their youth. You will need to know the kinds of foods they ate, what they were wearing, the games they played and be prepared to describe the smell of freshly cut grass or the aroma of buttercups. It is important to engage all the senses.

Adaptation: You could start off this activity by doing some relaxation exercises, such as Progressive Muscle Relaxation Exercises. You can find out more about this at www.parentsandfamilies.com. You may wish to incorporate props into this activity – such as using a picnic rug, if this is your theme – or creating the smell of freshly baked bread.

19 Family heirlooms

Description: Family 'treasures', passed down through the generations, provide a wonderful insight into our own personal history. Tactile interaction with a precious object – whether a baptismal gown, grandfather's watch or a photo of a relative on their wedding day – can conjure up deep emotions and connections in a way that images alone can't. Although the treasured family items may be passed down, the tragedy is that the stories behind them can get forgotten. Ask your loved one and other family members about their possessions from the past and capture their special stories.

Props and Preparation: Decide on where you will record the stories of your family heirlooms. It is a good idea to take pictures to go alongside each heirloom. This is a very important task for you to undertake as a family because, in the digital age, there is a real danger that we may literally lose touch with precious family objects.

Adaptation: Your local library, museum or historical society will have books and articles on historic clothing, furniture, jewellery and other artefacts to help you learn more about the history of your family heirlooms.

20

Con-versation starters

Conversation starters

It is often the case that people find it easier and more natural to reminisce whilst engaged in some kind of activity. This might be chatting whilst taking a walk in the garden, working on a hobby or listening to music. Reminiscing in this informal way – and using different kinds of sensory triggers, such as objects, photographs, smells, music and old-fashioned footage – will help your loved one to take delight in talking about their past. Many of the activities, described above, include ideas and pointers for reminiscence work, but here are a few more conversation starters:

- Cars that you have owned over the years: favourite cars and memories of special outings and trips behind the wheel

- Ways that you used to earn money: collecting rags, empty bottles and selling coal from an old pram or pushcart

- Trips to the dentist: the black rubber mask you had to wear for tooth extractions

- Memories of getting your first television set and the programmes you used to watch

- Items you used to collect, including postcards, cigarette cards, Matchbox toys and marbles

- Your most valuable possessions as a child – which were often kept in a small wooden or tin box

- The 'street games' of yesteryear: 'Queenie, queenie, who's got the ball?'

- How you used to dress for different occasions: both boys and girls used to wear a white sleeveless vest under their shirt or blouse

- How your bedroom used to look – without a TV or games console (and with a bed that doubled up as a trampoline)

- Remembering school days – including tuck shops, milk monitors, writing on slate boards and outside toilets

- Manners and etiquette: calling a teacher either 'Sir' or 'Madam', speaking when you're spoken to, never wearing a hat indoors, or when you were talking to a lady.

Conversation starters can also be visual.
Visit www.parentsandfamilies.com for 40 must-see photos from the past, which are bound to trigger memories and associations.

More reminiscence activities

21 Yesterday's news

Buy a newspaper from the past, or search online at the British Newspaper Archive. With the coffee freshly brewing, you can sit down to read the paper together or you can read out sections to your loved one to trigger memories from the past. How about getting hold of an edition from a significant event in their past or a memorable historical event? You can also use newspapers to research your family history. It isn't just the wealthy or famous who appear in newspapers!

22 Send a postcard

Imagine a time before social media, text messages, mobile phones and Skype. How did people actually communicate with each other? The answer: they wrote postcards and letters! Postcards are a brilliant way to capture and share memories. Stock up on old-fashioned postcards, and encourage your loved one to send a postcard to another family member, describing the activities they have enjoyed or a treasured memory they have remembered. There is also much enjoyment to be had looking through an old collection of postcards. It's not just the images on the cards, of a particular place in time, which are captivating; it's the story behind the hand-written messages.

23 Old annuals

No Christmas was complete without an annual, featuring the best of the year's stories, articles and illustrations from your favourite comic book. These books are real pieces of history, with their lavish design and colourful covers. Although many annuals fell out of production post-World War Two, when other forms of literature and entertainment took over, The Beano Annual has been published every year since 1939. Watch your loved one's face light up when you present them with a copy of a traditional annual – and spend time reading the comic strips and articles together.

24 Guess who?

An activity that calls upon your loved one's ability to recall people and events from the distant past is more likely to be successful than one that relies on short-term memory and remembering events from the more recent past. Compile a collage of family photos from your past and invite the family to guess who's who.

25 Family photos

We will all experience our memory fading over time, and we will all forget little details about our lives. Photographs are an important record of our personal history, a way to capture and preserve happy memories and a vital link to the people we love most in our lives. We should all consider writing the names of people on the back of the photograph, where they were taken and the date. Does your loved one have a favourite photograph from the past? How about recreating a modern-day equivalent of that favourite family 'pose'. This may involve a family outing to the original location that the old photograph was taken, if this is feasible – a great excuse for a trip down memory lane!

26 What comes next?

Old sayings and well-used expressions tend to stay with us because they are deeply embedded in our memory. This activity can either be played as a game or as a starting-point for reminiscence and conversation. Select some well-known sayings, traditional proverbs and nursery rhymes; read out the first part of the saying and ask your loved one to finish the saying. For example, 'a bird in the hand is worth … (two in the bush)'. As an alternative, you could type them out on paper or card and then physically match the two parts of the saying together. Visit www.parentsandfamilies.com for a link to a website that lists phrases and sayings and their origins.

27 Collections

Collecting has always been a popular childhood hobby. The true meaning of 'collecting' comes from building up 'keepsakes', which have a sentimental value and trigger fond memories. Your loved one may recall their treasured collections of stamps, postcards, Matchbox toys, marbles or cigarette cards. Collecting was always a sociable activity, with friends swapping things between each other to make up sets, or to pass on duplicates. Spend some time asking your loved one about what they used to collect and encourage your family generations to build up their own unique collection together.

28 Stoking up memories

There is nothing quite like relaxing and sitting around a campfire, toasting marshmallows, swapping stories and singing along to campfire songs. Even if you can't recreate the moment by heading outdoors and sitting around a campfire, with a little imagination you can sit around the fire indoors and enjoy some fireside traditions. Campfire songs that your loved one may remember include, 'Quartermaster's store' and 'Do your ears hang low'.

29
Visit a museum

Museums are a treasure-trove of sensory stimulation, reminiscence and learning for everyone. They are ideal places to trigger memories and handle objects from the past, helping to transport your loved one back in time. The great thing is, nowadays, you can visit the museum's website before you go and plan the focus of your visit. If your loved one has a particular interest in collectables, transport or even marbles, you can guarantee that somewhere you will find a museum collection that stimulates these interests. Don't try and do it all in one visit, though. You should plan for a visit of no more than two hours and factor in breaks to rest, relax and remember at the museum café.

30
Classic car show

For a true taste of nostalgia, you can't beat a classic car show or rally. It's a wonderful way to spend time, wandering around looking at cars from all eras, chatting to the owners about their history and perhaps enjoying an old-fashioned picnic, if the weather is fine. There are many events that happen all year round, so you are bound to find one local to you. In the run up to the show or rally, you could look through old Haynes manuals and start reminiscing about cars and travels from the past.

Ball games

Exercise can be beneficial for both the physical and mental health of a loved one with dementia. It can help with coordination, maintaining muscle strength and reducing the risk of falls. It is also a fantastic way to bring the generations together. With all the games mentioned below, you need to start from the person's abilities and consider their likes and dislikes. Please also check our website for guidance on exercise for people with underlying health problems, such as high blood pressure.

31
The 7-up game

Description: It is very likely that your parents and grandparents will remember the 7-up game from their childhood. The aim of the game is to bounce a ball against a wall (or throw a ball up in the air) a set number of times while performing a skill in between bounces, such as spinning around or throwing the ball under your leg. For a full list of rules, see www.parentsandfamilies.com or you can simply invent your own seven different ways of catching a ball.

Props and Preparation: This game does require following, and remembering, a set of instructions, which some people with dementia may find difficult. Be prepared to adapt this activity to a simple catching game, if it doesn't work out. You will also need to ensure that you have enough space to play 7-up safely.

Adaptation: You can't go wrong with a game of cup-and-ball. This is a wooden cup with a handle and a small ball attached to the cup by a string. The object of the exercise is to get the ball to land inside the cup. You can have a competition amongst family members to see who can score the most points.

32
Piggy in the middle

Description: This game requires three people. Two of you should stand about ten metres apart and the third person is the 'piggy' in the middle. The two players on the outside throw the ball to each other, whilst the one in the middle tries to catch it. If this happens, then the person who threw the ball that is intercepted becomes the 'piggy'.

Props and Preparation: This game requires very little preparation, but make sure you have plenty of space and nothing breakable in sight!

Adaptation: If this game is too much for your loved one, then it is worth investing in one of the many chair-based activity games, such as chair crazy golf or inflatable hoopla. You could also adapt this game by playing with a balloon, as opposed to a ball.

33 One knee, two knee

Description: This is another variation on a catching game. You throw the ball to each other and if you drop the ball you have to go on one knee, then two knees if you drop it again, then catch it with one elbow on the floor … You can make up your own rules if you like.

Props and Preparation: A fairly high degree of mobility is required for this game, so you may wish to follow the adaptation below.

Adaptation: Your loved one can stay in the chair to throw and catch the ball, whilst the rest of the family does all the actions!

34 Marbles

Description: Marbles is certainly a game that has stood the test of time, and there are many different games of marbles you can play. For example, 'Boss-out' is when one player rolls a marble and, when it stops, the second player tries to hit it with one of his. If he succeeds, he takes the original marble; if not, the first player gets the opportunity to roll a marble at his opponent's. 'Dropsies' is played in a square (about one metre by one metre) and each player has to put five marbles within the square. The idea is to drop your 'shooter' from above waist height so that it lands on one of your opponent's marbles and knocks it out of the square.

Props and Preparation: You can buy marbles from almost any toy store and you will find original, collectors' items on the internet. Most games require only a flat playing surface and perhaps some chalk or string to mark out the playing area. You can also make your own marble run, or cut out arches in a cereal packet, scoring different points for each arch that you aim your marble through.

Adaptation: Different types of marbles have different names – including 'steelies', 'cat's eyes' and 'oilies' – and you can spend time reminiscing with your loved one about these different names. Even if they are not able to participate in the games, they will enjoy holding and feeling the different weights and textures of the marbles, and perhaps sorting them into an old tin box or a traditional marbles pouch. Did you know that you can also play a game of solitaire with marbles?

Good old-fashioned games

Few things bring a family together like a good old-fashioned games night – and there are so many classic games loved by young and old alike. For the person with dementia, board games help with social interaction, taking the initiative, planning, coordination and focus, and they bring immediate pleasure to those taking part. Furthermore, board games are generally inexpensive and involve a wide range of tasks – from simple ones such as bingo, to complex ones such as chess. Games can be adapted to the abilities of all the players and there are so many to choose from. As well as the games described below, see if your loved one remembers: The Popular Game of Magnetic Fishing, The Amazing Magic Robot, Sorry and L'Attaque, to name but a few. These are all games that you can still get hold of today.

35 Tiddlywinks

Description: Tiddlywinks is played on a flat surface (usually on a felt mat), with sets of small disks, called 'winks', and a pot. The object of the game is to score points by landing your winks into the pot, using a larger disk to flick them up in the air. Believe it or not, tiddlywinks can be highly competitive, and the modern game originated from a group of Cambridge University students, who wanted to devise a sport for which they could represent the university!

Props and Preparation: You can purchase a tiddlywinks set in almost any toy shop. Many sets use replica packaging from the 1950s and 1960s, which will add to the nostalgia of playing tiddlywinks.

Adaptation: Many of the shots in tiddlywinks have acquired their own unusual names, some of which have become dictionary entries! See www.parentsandfamilies.com for tiddlywinks terminology and reminisce with your loved one about the games they remember. If your loved one doesn't want to engage with the game, then they may enjoy simply sorting the tiddlywinks into the different colours and sizes.

36 Pick up Sticks

Description: Pick up Sticks will help to improve dexterity, coordination and concentration. It is also a brilliant reminder of childhood and a simple game to play. Pick up all the sticks in a bundle and then release them, so that they end up in a jumbled pile. The aim of the game is to remove a stick from the pile without moving any other sticks. Your turn continues until you make a mistake and the game ends when all the sticks have been picked up.

Props and Preparation: You can buy an original Pick up Sticks game or get a larger, chunkier version, so the sticks are easier to handle and grip.

Adaptation: As with almost any game, you can simplify the rules yourself to make the game easier to play and the instructions easier to follow. For example, you could reduce the number of sticks or simply take it in turns to pick up one stick at a time.

37 Jacks

Description: Jacks is another example of a game that has been around for centuries and that will evoke childhood memories. There are many different variations to the game, but it generally involves scattering the 'jacks' on a surface and then throwing a ball in the air and attempting to pick up the jacks before the ball bounces.

Props and Preparation: You could actually make your own version of jacks, if you didn't want to buy a copy. In China and Japan, they play a similar game using cloth bags filled with rice, sand or beans. This is something you could easily make as a family. With this version, you drop all the bags on the table, bar one. You toss that bag up in the air and attempt to pick up one of the others before the bag lands. Keeping the bags you have already picked up in one hand, you then attempt to pick up the remaining bags in the same way.

Adaptation: There are many other games that you can play as a family and plenty of places where you can buy old-fashioned games. See www.parentsandfamilies.com for more game-based inspiration.

38 Matchstick tower

Description: This is a great example of a home-made game! Get a pile of matchsticks, and see how many you can place on top of an egg cup before they start to fall off. Hint: lay the matches in a diamond or square to start and then add more matchsticks from there. You can play against each other, with each team having their own egg cup and pile of matches. Who can keep going the longest?

Props and Preparation: All you need for this game is a pile of matchsticks and an egg cup!

Adaptation: How many games can you invent as a family? You could base your family game on an existing one, such as dominoes, and replace the dots with old-fashioned pictures, for example.

39

Board games

Description: There is nothing quite like gathering around a board game, and this is what families used to do for an evening's entertainment. As well as trying your luck, testing your strategy, improving your concentration and learning new things, there is the simple, tactile pleasure to be had in physically moving pieces around a board, picking up cards, rolling dice and performing actions. Many of the board games that were invented in the 1950s and 1960s are still popular today. As a family, how about spending a nostalgic evening playing Beetle, Yahtzee, Bucaneer, Kerplunk, Risk, Ludo, Battleships, Game of Life or Cluedo?

Props and Preparation: You will need to decide on the games you are going to play, based on your loved one's abilities and interests. Remember that the person with dementia may have difficulty following instructions, so make sure you understand the rules yourself and use one-step, simple instructions when explaining the game.

Adaptation: You can often buy large-format games, such as a giant Connect 4, that you can play in the garden. This allows you to combine playing games with exercise, bringing additional benefits to the intergenerational activity.

Old party games

Party games from the past offer an opportunity to reminisce and join in the fun and laughter associated with games. Remember that although a person with dementia may forget the facts and 'details' of the party games, the feelings of enjoyment and contentment will stay with them after the fun has finished. It is worth offering some words of caution about parties, however. Try and avoid over-stimulation and having too much going on, as this could cause some distress for your loved one. Play one game at a time and factor in some quiet time afterwards to rest and have a cup of tea. Remember that it doesn't matter if they don't play the games right – and it won't help if you try and correct them!

40
Pass the parcel

Description: Pass the parcel is perhaps the most played of all party games. Everyone sits in a circle, within reach of each other, and you pass around a pre-wrapped gift until the music stops. The person holding the parcel when the music stops gets to remove one layer of wrapping and you continue starting and stopping the music until the last person removes the final layer of wrapping and discovers their gift.

Props and Preparation: Make sure you choose music that your loved one will enjoy and remember from their past. Rather than using lots of wrapping paper, you can always use newspaper instead.

Adaptation: To add interest to the game, you could add some simple, funny challenges to each layer of wrapping paper. You could even write out some reminiscence questions or quiz questions and add these to the layers of the parcel. Even if your loved one doesn't want to partake in this game, they will enjoy watching the reactions on everyone else's faces.

41
Bucket toss

Description: Versions of this simple game were popular at carnivals in the past. Set up a few different-sized buckets or pots, filled with prizes if you wish. Mark a line that you must not cross. The object of the game is to stand behind the line and throw a ping pong ball so that it lands in the bucket. Alternatively, you can get a large piece of plywood and paint on a face of a clown. Make holes for his mouth, nose and clown hat and decide on points for each hole. The aim of this game is to throw a beanbag, so that it goes through one of the holes.

Props and Preparation: You will need to purchase some plywood (or thick cardboard) and some brightly coloured paint to make your own clown board. For some instructions, go to www.parentsandfamilies.com.

Adaptation: For a simpler version, get hold of a large jar and some old-fashioned clothes pegs. Children can stand on a chair so that they are the same height as the adults, and then they must try to drop the clothes pegs into the jar. It is worth looking for some old-fashioned dolly pegs, as these could well spark off some reminiscence about wash days and home life from days gone by. Furthermore, you can use the dolly pegs to create your own 'dollies', as described in the 'Crafty ways' on page 56.

42 Musical statues

Description: Musical statues combines music and dance – two activities that help to improve the well-being of people with dementia. When we engage with music – and respond to it by dancing – we actually have to do little or no mental processing. For this reason, it is an ideal activity for someone with dementia. The rules for this activity are very simple: when the music starts, you dance around to the music, and when the music stops, you freeze in the position you happen to be in. One person in the family should be the judge and see who is still moving, or who doesn't stop fast enough, and that person is called out of the game. You keep going until there is only one person left: the winner.

Props and Preparation: Make sure you pick the right music. Look for songs that use percussion and have fairly quick tempos, which will naturally encourage movement.

Adaptation: Musical statues doesn't have to be a competition, it can just be an alternative way of dancing together by incorporating stopping with the music. If you want to take the game further, then you can call a theme for the statues, getting people to impersonate different animals, for example.

Healthy competition

Games should primarily be played for stimulation and enjoyment, not for competition. Competition can be stressful for someone living with dementia because it puts pressure on them to find the right answer, react quickly or remember a strict set of rules. On the other hand, games can provide mental stimulation and promote a sense of teamwork and belonging. The most successful games will work on several levels and engage all the senses. They will include colourful, tactile objects that can be handled and a kinesthetic element, involving movement and music. Above all else, the most successful games are those that your loved one has chosen to play, and that will stimulate memories from their childhood.

43 Bingo

Description: Bingo is not only a very popular game but, when played with high-contrast, large bingo cards, researchers have found that it helps to improve the visual perception problems experienced by those with mild dementia. If your loved one has always enjoyed bingo, then this is a fail-safe activity, as it will tap into their long-term memory. You can either buy a bingo set or make your own.

Props and Preparation: It is a good idea to buy a set of large-print bingo cards, and use counters instead of crossing numbers off with a pen. This will help to make the game more tactile and engaging.

Adaptation: There are plenty of variations of bingo. There is musical bingo, where you cross off the names of the well-known songs that you hear, and a bingo game using images instead of numbers. How about making your own famous faces bingo game, using photographs of famous people from the past?

44 Name that tune

Description: Music can soothe, stimulate and trigger long-forgotten memories. The area of the brain associated with musical patterns seems to remain responsive even after speech starts to fail. This may be why someone who struggles to string a sentence together can sing all the right words to a familiar song in the right order.

Props and Preparation: You can buy musical quiz games or devise your own, whereby you play the first few bars of a song and you either have to name the tune or sing the next line of music.

Adaptation: Remember that it's not about the competitive element of this game. If your loved one would prefer a good old sing-along then be guided by what they want to do.

45 Talent contests

Description: A knobbly knees competition will bring memories flooding back of the heyday of traditional holiday camps. Large, seaside holiday camps were very popular during the 1950s, and everything was in the name of organised fun. You may wish to consider planning your own holiday-camp style entertainment – particularly if you have a large family gathering coming up. As well as the knobbly knees competition, activities included the wheelbarrow race, bonny baby contest, glamorous grannies, doing the conga and the three-legged race.

Props and Preparation: You will want to choose your activities wisely – and have a mix of more sedate activities (bingo was also popular at holiday camps) with physically active ones. If time and enthusiasm permits, it is a good idea for the children in the family to come up with, and perform, their own talent show.

Adaptation: There is a lot of history about holiday camps on the internet and your loved one may recall favourite family holidays. Spend some time looking at old photographs, entertainment programmes and advertising posters on the internet and reminisce about time spent on holiday.

46

Mimes

Description: This activity is a different take on the game of charades. One of the great things about it is that you can adapt the words you act out to suit the interests and abilities of everyone you are playing with. All you need to do is prepare some cards with the name of a job, task or activity written on. Simply take turns acting out the name on the card, with everyone else guessing.

Props and Preparation: Some suggestions to write on the cards: serving in tennis, tossing a pancake, eating spaghetti, being chased by a wasp, avoiding puddles and riding a horse. You can make the activities as humorous as you like – and children are bound to come up with some very imaginative ideas.

Adaptation: You can decide on a winner – such as the first person to guess five words correctly – or play just for fun.

Retro toys

Providing your loved one with a range of retro toys from their past will trigger memories and encourage activity. Memories from the most recent past tend to be lost first, so toys from childhood will be recognisable, and provide comfort and familiarity. Retro toys help to take people back to a place where they feel at ease. There are many retro toys that your loved one will remember: Spirograph, Tinkertoy and Etch-a-sketch to name but a few.

47

Spinning top

Description: The spinning top is one of the world's oldest toys. There is something very therapeutic and mesmerising about watching a spinning top balance and spin on its tiny tip. The different shades and designs add to the hypnotic effect as you watch the colours of the toy swirl into one. It is both a toy to 'play' with and a distraction to calm and ease agitation. Someone with dementia may fidget constantly, so having something to occupy their hands, like a spinning top, can help.

Props and Preparation: There are many different types of spinning top that you can buy. These range from classic wooden ones with string (a bit more of a challenge), wooden ones and pump-action ones. On www.parentsandfamilies.com, you can even find a document that tells you the history of spinning tops.

Adaptation: Take part in International Top Spinning Day, which usually takes place every October! You can also make your own – using a piece of card and a matchstick – and have a family competition to see who can spin theirs for the longest!

48 Cup-and-ball

Description: Cup-and-ball is a traditional children's toy, consisting of a small wooden ball connected to a handle of a cup by a piece of string. The player has to toss the ball upwards and attempt to catch the ball in the cup. If they succeed, they get a point, and the idea is to see how many times in a row you can land the ball in the cup.

Props and Preparation: A traditional cup-and-ball is inexpensive and can be bought either online or in a toy shop.

Adaptation: It is relatively straightforward to make your own version of this game – although it won't quite have the same reminiscence value! All you need is a paper cup, aluminium foil, string and a stick or pencil. There are full instructions at www.parentsandfamilies.com.

49 Skipping rope

Description: Skipping ropes were very popular and your loved one is bound to remember using the washing line for something long enough to skip as a group. The rope would be turned by one person at either end and the turners would get the rope to slap the pavement in time to the rhythm of the rhyme being chanted by the skippers. The skippers would do tricks such as running out from the turning rope, and rejoining without missing a beat.

Props and Preparation: Skipping can easily become a family activity and all you need is a long rope and plenty of space to swing it. It's best to start with simply jumping over the rope before you try any fancy tricks!

Adaptation: If your loved one isn't able to join in, they can help to turn the skipping rope. Alternatively, you could run a reminiscence session on the many skipping rhymes that were popular back in the day. You can find a list of some rhymes at www.parentsandfamilies.com.

50
Table skittles

Description: Table skittles is a traditional game that has been played for centuries in pubs and inns, and it came about when pub landlords wanted to devise a miniature version of traditional skittles so that the game could be played on a tabletop. Nine small skittles are positioned on a square, and the objective is to knock over all the skittles by swinging a ball, which hangs on a chain from a pole positioned on the board.

Props and Preparation: In order to play this game, you will need to purchase your own table skittles set.

Adaption: If one of the family gets really good at this game, then they can join a local table skittle league!

51
Yo-yo

Description: The yo-yo has been around for centuries and is certainly a universal toy. It became particularly popular throughout the 1930s, '40s and '50s when the toy was promoted, using innovative demonstrations and contests. All of the classic yo-yo tricks were developed during this period. As well as being a toy for learning tricks – and even entering competitions – there is something very relaxing and calming about playing with a yo-yo, which your loved one is likely to benefit from. It is another example of a retro toy that provides a welcome distraction from anxiety and sensory overload.

Props and Preparation: In recent years, technology has influenced a plethora of the products we use, and not even the seemingly simple yo-yo has escaped. They come in all different shapes with different axles – some of which are more suitable for tricks than others. The traditional yo-yo is the 'imperial' shape, which is the one your loved one is most likely to recognise.

Adaptation: Yo-yoing can easily become a popular family pastime, and the beauty of it is you can all develop your skills with the yo-yo at your own pace. Visit www.parentsandfamilies.com for a link to the different tricks you can learn – from Walk the Dog to Around the World.

More games

52
Noughts and crosses

The game, noughts and crosses, has been around for centuries. In fact, there is evidence that it was first played by the ancient Egyptians in around 1300 BC. In 1952, it was the first game to ever be played on a computer. The beauty of this game lies in its simplicity. All you need is paper and a pen (or even chalk and an old slate board), or you can buy a wooden version of the game or even a giant one to play in the garden. Please note that your loved one may know this game as tic-tac-toe, its old-fashioned name.

53
Dominoes

Dominoes is an ideal game to play as a family as the rules are easy to follow and the game will be familiar to your loved one. Dominoes can help a person with dementia improve their dexterity and coordination and utilise their ability to match objects. You begin by placing all the dominoes face down on the table, and each player takes seven dominoes to form their 'hand'. The object of the game is for players to get rid of all their dominoes, matching them end-to-end with those already out in play on the table. You can alter the rules to make it simpler for your loved one and you can buy different versions of the game, with colours and shapes as opposed to different number dots.

54
Games compendium

Toys and games these days are so much more technology-based, anti-social and focused on instant gratification. On the other hand, the games of yesteryear got everyone involved, ensured quality family time and were great fun. Most families used to own a classic games compendium, which brought together all your favourite games in one place, usually housed within a neat wooden box where the lid doubled as a chess board. There was chess, draughts, backgammon, dominoes, solitaire, snakes and ladders and tiddlywinks, along with counters and dice. Purchasing an old-fashioned games compendium will not only evoke memories but also bring a new meaning to family interaction and entertainment.

55
Card Games

In order to choose which card games to play with your loved one, opt for games where they already know the rules or where the rules are easy to follow. Popular card games from the past include Patience, Rummy, Old Maid, Go Fish, Newmarket and Snap. Remember that if your loved one had no interest in playing cards in the past, then it is unlikely that they will now. However, you could try sorting the cards into suits or colours if your loved one's dementia is in the mid to late stages. Just touching and looking at the cards is likely to stimulate memories and lead to some reminiscence.

56 Jigsaw puzzles

Sitting around the kitchen table completing a jigsaw puzzle is a popular family activity in many households. What is more, this simple activity brings brain-boosting benefits. Jigsaws help to improve hand-eye coordination, focus, concentration and recognition. There is also the sense of satisfaction and achievement of completing the puzzle. It is possible to obtain jigsaw puzzles specifically designed for people with dementia, with fewer pieces and based on themes of everyday life, which stimulate discussion.

57 Make your own puzzle

Make a jigsaw puzzle, unique to your family, that no-one else will have. Start by finding a photograph or picture (about twelve inches square). You may need to get your photograph enlarged in order for it to be suitable for a puzzle. Choose the type of backing – whether foam, heavy cardboard or a thin sheet of wood – and stick your photograph to this backing. Once you have finished the mounting and allowed the glue to set, then you can set about cutting your new jigsaw puzzle into different interlocking shapes. Some photo printing companies offer this as a service if you send a digital version of your photo.

58 Cat's cradle

Cat's cradle is a string game that has been played all over the world for centuries. All you need is a piece of string or wool, looped and tied together at the ends. This game is designed to be played by two people and the aim is to make different 'figures' (or configurations) with the string. For full instructions, visit www.parentsandfamilies.com.

59 Play dough

Whilst you should go to great lengths to ensure that this activity is not perceived as 'childish' by your loved one, creating play dough models can be a great activity for all the family. Play-Doh was first launched commercially on the toy market in the mid-1950s, so it's likely to bring back childhood and family-time memories. You can make your own play dough by following the recipe at www.parentsandfamilies.com. As an alternative to using play dough, how about making figures and decorations out of marzipan, which can then be used on cakes or as gifts for the family? Using marzipan in this way has the same sensory benefits as play dough – but with a meaningful use for your creations at the end.

60 The Tangle

Whilst this isn't technically an activity for all the family to engage in together, the Tangle is an innovative toy that you can twist and move around in a continuous motion. It is suitable – and addictive – for all ages, but it is particularly beneficial for someone with dementia who finds it relaxing to have something to occupy their hands. Twisting and turning the Tangle will help the joints in the hands, provide tactile stimulation, and create a state of calmness. To find out more about the Tangle, visit www.parentsandfamilies.com.

61 Table tennis

According to research, table tennis activates multiple areas of the brain simultaneously, thus providing a 'brain workout' as well as a physical workout. It truly is a game for all ages and improves alertness, balance and coordination. In fact, of all the sports, table tennis has been singled out as providing benefits for people with dementia. You don't need an expensive table tennis table to play, as you can purchase kits with moveable nets, which can be attached to any table.

62 Play (magnetic) darts

If your loved one has always enjoyed playing darts, then reintroduce it as a family game. Playing darts not only encourages interaction and repartee between family members, but it also helps retain hand-eye coordination. It may well also lead to stories about pub teams and infamous matches. Don't be frustrated if your loved one can't keep track of the score, it really is the taking part that counts! Rather than using the traditional dartboard, you can buy magnetic darts or those with Velcro tips. This is a better, and safer, option for playing darts inside your house.

63 Playing quoits

Quoits is a traditional game that involves throwing rings over a set distance and trying to get them to land over one or more spikes. There are many different versions of this game – but the version you are most likely to play is garden quoits, or hoopla. A hoopla set can be purchased from shops and consists of rope hoops that must be thrown over wooden spikes, all with different point scores.

64 Bagatelle

Bagatelle is an indoor table game, where the idea is to get a number of balls past nails, which act as obstacles, into different holes (which are all worth different points). The balls are generally shot from the bottom of the wooden board, using a similar action to that of a pinball machine. Playing bagatelle relies on luck, rather than skill, and the great thing about games of this type is that everyone has the same chance of succeeding.

65 Shove ha'penny

Shove ha'penny (or shove halfpenny) is another example of an old-fashioned game that can still be purchased today. The game is played on a wooden board, using old ha'penny coins. The object of the game is to 'shunt' your ha'penny up the board and get it to land in between the lines, or grooves, which run horizontally along the board. Even if your loved one is unable to join in the game, they will appreciate the feel of the smooth, wooden board and the old coins – and enjoy watching the rest of the family get competitive.

66 Remote-control car

What is not fun about racing a remote control car? Not only does this activity help improve hand-eye coordination and fine motor skills – since you are operating the control with your fingers – but it can easily be adapted depending on how advanced your loved one's dementia is. Grandparents, parents and children can make their own obstacle course – capitalising on the opportunity for some time building things in the shed – or buy two cars and have races. If your loved one's dementia is in the moderate to late stages, then look for cars with simpler controls.

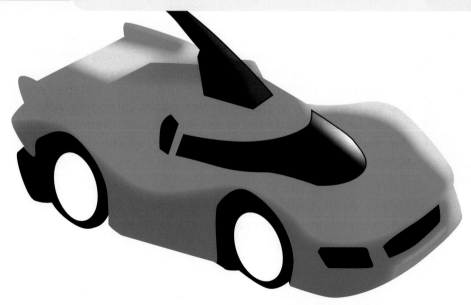

For the boys (or girls)

The men in your family, just like the women, will have a variety of skills, abilities, work history and interests. It is therefore impossible to take a one-size-fits-all approach. Many of the activities in this book will be of interest to both genders – such as the games, memory lane trips, technology-based activities, and gardening to name but a few. However, it doesn't hurt to come up with some activity ideas that will truly appeal to men.

67 Model Making

Description: Model-making kits come in all kinds of different shapes and sizes: model aircraft, model boats and doll's house furniture, to name but a few. They also come in a variety of skill levels, from those you just snap together to customised kits. The level of skill required is usually marked on the box. As well as putting the model together, take the opportunity to reminisce. For example, building a model of a World War Two plane could lead to talking about memories of the War.

Props and Preparation: Make sure that you match your loved one's ability, concentration span and interest to the type of model-making kit you select.

Adaptation: If it's too much to put the kit together, then your loved one can always help out with painting the model. Model-making doesn't have to involve wood or plastics! For a truly multi-sensory experience, you can purchase a chocolate model-making kit. See www.parentsandfamilies.com for more information.

68 Guy Fawkes

Description: Bonfire Night used to be known as Guy Fawkes Night, and children used to make stuffed 'guys', take them out on the streets and ask for a 'penny for the guy' to pay for fireworks. This is a great seasonal, intergenerational activity, and a chance to reminisce about Bonfire Night. Children used to start planning for Bonfire Night well in advance – collecting wood and old clothes as far back as September. This can be an activity that stretches over a couple of months!

Props and Preparation: You will need a sack (for the body), straw and/or newspaper (for the stuffing), string, a needle and cotton, four old stockings or football socks, a small bag (for the head), a mask for the face (or you can use papier mâché to make your own) and some old clothes. Begin by stuffing the sack for the body – using straw or tight balls of newspaper – putting a long stick in the sack before you close it to keep it rigid. Stuff four stockings, long socks or a pair of tights (for the legs) and a small bag for the head.

Sew the head, arms and legs on to the body, or tie them on with string. Lastly, add your mask or papier mâché face and dress him with old clothes and a funny hat.

Adaptation: Another Bonfire Night tradition was to wrap potatoes up in tin foil and place them in the fire to cook. Although you may not have an open fire, you can recreate the memory of holding a hot potato in your warm hand whilst watching the bonfire by serving up oven-baked jacket potatoes in tin foil. The night before Bonfire Night was known as 'Mischief Night', when children used to play practical jokes on grown-ups – and this presents another opportunity to reminisce. If it's not possible to make it out to a fireworks display, then sparklers in the garden can be magical.

69
Meccano

Description: Meccano was invented in 1898 by Frank Hornby, who wanted to create a system of parts, nuts and bolts to allow his two young boys to build working models and mechanical devices. Meccano model construction kits are all based on the principles of mechanical engineering, making this activity an ideal one if your loved one's working life involved some kind of engineering. It is more than just a 'toy' as it teaches how things are constructed and function.

Props and Preparation: You can construct practically anything using a Meccano kit – including dumper trucks, cranes, clocks, radio-controlled racing cars and even a model of Tower Bridge in London! The kits you can buy today include all the tools you need for assembly – but your loved one may have a preferred spanner or screwdriver they would like to use.

Adaptation: Meccano comes in varying levels of difficulty, so you can pick your kit according to ability. Alternatively, there is a wealth of memorabilia on the internet, and plenty of Meccano enthusiasts' pages, so you can spend time looking at pictures of Meccano models and reminiscing.

70

Men and sheds

Description: A shed is a place for mending, making, inventing, sorting, repairing, tinkering, sanding, carving, potting, planting and contemplating! For many men, it can be therapeutic to potter around doing odd jobs, and an intergenerational activity revolving around the shed can bring real purpose, meaning and enjoyment. There are many activities you can do together – from simply sitting in the shed and sorting nuts and bolts, to taking part in work-like activities, such as making a photoframe, painting a birdbox or varnishing wood.

Props and Preparation: You may wish to consider sourcing a collection of old tools to look at and handle – such as old planes, hammers, drill bits and handsaws. Even if you don't have a shed, there are still 'shed-based' activities you can replicate – including sanding wood, varnishing and organising drill bits. As a family, you may like to make up your own toolbox, containing items such as a tape measure, large nuts and bolts, a screwdriver, etc. As well as being practical and useful for activities, these items will serve as a basis for reminiscence.

Adaptation: Simply being in the environment of a shed can bring memories flooding back. You could spend some time sitting with a cup of tea, whilst listening to an old radio station and stimulating the senses through the familiar smells of oils, timber and sawdust. There are many other purposeful activities you can do, linked to daily routine, such as checking the rain gauge and thermometer.

Crafty ways

Making things brings a sense of accomplishment for everyone involved, which is why craft-based activities can have such a positive impact on your loved one's self-esteem. What is more, craft activities have a genuine sense of purpose, since what you make together can be used as a gift, a room decoration, a toy or to serve some other practical purpose. Remember that it doesn't matter how the end result turns out, what matters is the fun you have in getting creative and the resulting feelings of enjoyment and achievement. If your loved one's dementia is in the moderate to late stages, then learning new skills will be difficult – but you can tap into their existing knowledge of crafts they have always done, such as knitting, French knitting or crocheting.

71

French knitting

Description: French knitting, or spool knitting, is a timeless tradition that your loved one is bound to recall learning as a child. It produces a narrow tube of knitted fabric that you can then use to make lots of different things, like mats and knitted bracelets. You can buy French knitting dolls or make your own by fixing four nails into an old wooden cotton reel.

Props and Preparation: Old wooden cotton reels aren't easy to come by, but if you are lucky enough to find one, then all you need to do is hammer in four nails so that they make a square. You begin by threading the wool through the centre hole of the cotton wheel, before twisting the wool around each nail and pulling it taut. You then take the wool around the outside of the next nail, pick up the loop with a blunt needle and lift it over the nail. Repeat this sequence, working your way around the other nails, until you start to see your knitted tube appear through the hole in the cotton wheel.

Adaptation: You can either simply knit a long trail of cord or you can create something specific using a French knitting technique. See www.parentsandfamilies.com for some inspiration and for a more detailed description of the French knitting technique.

72

Making pompoms

Description: This activity is a fantastic introduction to crafts for children – and there aren't too many fiddly bits to get frustrated with. It will also tap into your loved one's memory of crafts as this creative activity has been around for a long time. To create a pompom, you firstly need to cut out two doughnut-shaped pieces of cardboard (about three inches across) and place them on top of each other. Wind wool through the centre and round both the cardboard rings, completing the last few rounds with a needle, until the hole is too small for the needle to fit through. You then need to cut the wool around the edges, between the two rings. Tie a piece of strong thread between the rings and knot it tightly. You can leave a bit of wool thread so you can hang the pompom ball up or attach it to something. Lastly, pull the cardboard away from the pompom and fluff out the ball.

Props and Preparation: You will need some cardboard, brightly coloured wool, a needle, some thread and a pair of scissors.

Adaptation: Don't limit yourself to making pompoms! Using this technique, you can create bobble hats, a pompom scarf, pompom animals, a rug, a garland and pompom bookmarks.

73

Decorating eggs

Description: This is what Easter eggs always used to be about! You may not be able to eat them, but they will look lovely hung on a traditional 'Easter tree', or as a personal Easter gift. Choose white eggs and wash them carefully. With a pin, make a hole at the pointed end of the egg, for blowing through, and a larger one at the other end, for the inside of the egg to come out. You then need to gently blow the egg out of the shell into a cup. Now, you are ready to decorate your egg.

Props and Preparation: Choose some paints or gather some craft bits and pieces to decorate your egg.

Adaptation: See www.parentsandfamilies.com for more ideas on colouring your eggs using red onions, cranberry juice and turmeric and real flowers! You could also incorporate an Easter egg hunt into this activity – whether inside or outside.

74

Proggy mats

Description: Proggy mats are basically rugs made from rags. There are different names for these rugs in different parts of the country, so your loved one may know them as clip mats or peg mats, for example. They were an economical option to keep feet warm in the days before carpets, and used to be made from old clothes and blankets and a sack. You would poke the strips of fabric through the sack using a 'progger'. Making proggy mats is an ideal craft-based project to enjoy with your loved one. Why stop at mats or rugs? You could also make wall-hangings, cushions or padded seats!

Props and Preparation: There are step-by-step instructions on how to make proggy mats at www.parentsandfamilies.com.

Adaptation: Rug-making was born out of necessity during the austerity years; they weren't simply used as decorative items! It is fascinating to talk to your loved one about ways to 'make do and mend'. Did you know that in the 1940s, leaflets were delivered to households calling on people to 'be imaginative' with potatoes and potatoes were even an ingredient in Christmas puddings! What other ways to 'make do and mend' does your loved one remember?

75

Peg dolls

Description: The tradition of making dolls from wooden clothes pegs comes from a time when families couldn't afford to buy toy dolls. When toy-making stopped during World War Two, children would imaginatively make toys from items they found in and around the home. Peg dolls are a perfect example of this. All you need is an old-fashioned peg and then you can design your own peg doll using almost anything you like. You will find lots of ideas and inspiration at www.parentsandfamilies.com.

Props and Preparation: You will need to buy some old-fashioned wooden 'dolly pegs', which are not difficult to get hold of. You should then collect things like scraps of fabric for the dress (with a small length of cotton to create a waist for the doll), pipe cleaners for the arms, beads and sequins to decorate the dress, wool for the hair, and you can even make skirts for the doll out of cupcake cases! In addition, you will need glue, scissors and felt tip pens. It is a good idea to coat the peg in clear nail varnish to stop the ink from seeping into the wood when you draw on the face.

Adaptation: You could choose a theme for your peg dolls – such as making superheroes, jungle animals or mermaids. You could even create a 'set' for your dolls and use this as a basis for some story-telling. There are endless ways of using a craft theme to encourage meaningful, intergenerational activities. How about making a resolution as a family to give each other at least one home-made gift every holiday? Children could be encouraged to write, or blog, about what they achieve.

Festive fun

Going back to a traditional Christmas means making Christmas gifts, finding logs and fir cones for decorations, real wax candles on Christmas trees (which wouldn't pass the Health and Safety test nowadays!), decorating the house with garlands and Christmas lanterns, singing Christmas carols and Christmas stockings with symbolic gifts – such as a shiny new penny to signify wealth. The activities that follow are all based on making decorations and gifts, as was customary in the austerity years.

76
Making paper chains

Description: Christmas paper chains are traditional decorations that are easy to make. Once you start, you will find it difficult to stop! The fact that there are no complicated instructions to follow, and it relies on a repetitive action, makes it an ideal activity for your loved one. To make paper chains, first cut strips of coloured or patterned paper. Fold one strip into a loop and stick the ends together. Thread the next one through the first and stick together as before. Keep going until your chain is as long as you want it to be.

Props and Preparation: You can either cut the strips for paper chains yourself or you can buy ready-made strips from shops (which won't require the use of glue).

Adaptation: As well as making paper chains, you can make paper angels by creating a template and cutting out this shape on a folded piece of paper. You can find further instructions at www.parentsandfamilies.com.

77
Sewing cards

Description: Sewing cards, or lacing cards, involve threading a piece of wool or lace around the outline of an image or following the holes in a pattern. It is like dot-to-dot but with laces, rather than a pen. Dementia affects fine motor skills, and the ability to complete tasks that require hand-eye coordination, but this activity is easily simplified by using bigger pictures with fewer holes.

Props and preparation: Whilst it is still possible to buy sewing cards, you can easily make your own as a family project. Find appropriate pictures that will appeal to your loved one, laminate them and then use a hole punch to create a pattern.

Adaptation: To make this activity all the more purposeful, set the task of creating gift cards using this technique.

78
Paper snowflakes

Description: Paper snowflakes are another easy-to-make, traditional decoration. All you need is paper and scissors and you are good to go. They can be stuck to the window or hung from the ceiling.

Props and Preparation: For instructions on how to make the perfect paper snowflake, visit www.parentsandfamilies.com.

Adaptation: If you are feeling really adventurous as a family, then you can make a 3D paper snowflake. Alternatively, you can glue your snowflake on to a card for a personalised gift.

79
Twine stars

Description: For a rustic Christmas decoration, make a twine-wrapped Christmas star. Start by creating a hollow star shape, using either thick cardboard or lolly sticks glued together. Glue the end of some garden twine or some string to one of the 'V's of the star, and start winding your twine around, gluing as you go. Save all the tips of the star for last, and then, beginning at the top (and securing the end of the twine with glue), work your way down each tip. Finally, you can then glue on a hanging hook and add any decorations you wish

Props and Preparation: There is very little preparation for this activity and it is ideal for teamwork, sharing the tasks of starting off the winding around the star and the tips, with the main task of winding the twine around the body of the star. For visual instructions for this activity, visit www.parentsandfamilies.com.

Adaptation: Smaller versions of twine stars make lovely Christmas gifts. Did you know that it always used to be a working-class tradition to disguise gifts? For example, an embroidered handkerchief may have been folded inside a matchbox and hung on the Christmas tree.

Getting arty

The creative part of the brain is one of the last areas to be affected by dementia, so it follows that any activity that encourages creative expression will be both rewarding and enjoyable. It is also true to say that the most successful activities are those that don't have any sense of failure and you can't get anything 'wrong' with art. The activities below allow people to go at their own pace and provide an outlet for communication and expression when finding the right words may be more difficult. As if you needed any more convincing of the wonder of creativity, according to some recent research by Arts 4 Dementia (2013), 94 per cent of people with dementia were energised, unstressed, happy and alert for at least 24 hours after an arts session.

80

Tile painting

Description: Plain ceramic tiles provide a blank canvas on which to allow your creative side to run freely! Almost anything goes with this activity, although you may wish to set a theme, such as the sea or farm animals. Individuals in mid-to-late stage dementia often respond best to brightly coloured paints, but you could equally use scraps of materials to add texture to your tile design.

Props and Preparation: All you will need for this activity is a few ceramic tiles, some acrylic paints and some clear acrylic spray to spray the tile when your design is complete.

Adaptation: Painted tiles make great gifts, such as coasters. Alternatively, how about creating a family mural, with each member of the family painting their own tile? You could each decide to paint something that is symbolic to your family, so you end up with a family 'coat of arms'. This can then be displayed inside or outside the home.

81

Making mosaics

Description: Mosaic is the art of creating pictures using small pieces of coloured glass, stone or other materials. In this activity, we are going to focus on using different textiles to make a mosaic, as this brings added benefits. You may notice that your loved one gravitates towards exploring the fabric of their clothing or the smoothness of the table. This is because exploring different textures aids relaxation, and the sense of touch requires little cognitive interpretation to be fully appreciated. Furthermore, many people with dementia have a need to be doing something with their hands and enjoying a textile mosaic will bring a feeling of calmness. Start by identifying as many different textures of material as possible – including fur, velvet, jute and wool. Cut up the materials into small pieces and decide on the design you want to create. You can then either glue or sew on the different textured pieces to a base to create the pattern.

Props and Preparation: Search around at home for different pieces of material, or visit a haberdashery. You don't want to cut the pieces too small as you still want your loved one to properly appreciate the changes in texture as they rub their hands over it. This is an activity that can be done together, or which children can take on themselves as a present for their loved one.

Adaptation: As a quirky, crafty alternative, did you know that you can use egg shells to make a mosaic? This is far safer than breaking up bits of tiles. Start by painting eggshells with craft paint, before gluing on your design. For more information, go to www.parentsandfamilies.com.

82 Just add water

Description: Just imagine if you could 'magically' produce a work of art using just a paintbrush and some water. Well, you can! 'Magic Painting Books' have been around for years and, if you are really lucky, you may be able to pick up an original, vintage book. As soon as water is applied to a seemingly blank piece of paper, a picture is magically revealed.

Props and Preparation: There are many different kinds of magic painting books on the market. Look for one where the theme is likely to appeal to your loved one, as this type of creative activity is also an excellent springboard for reminiscence.

Adaptation: Activities need to be one-step, repetitive and simple when dementia progresses, and the repetitive movement of the brush strokes in this activity can be therapeutic. You may need to start the brush movement, if your loved one is struggling.

83 Seed pictures

Description: Seed art is an old craft going back many years. The fun to be had in collecting seeds as a family – and seeing who can find the greatest variety – is matched by the enjoyment in creating your seed picture. You can use sunflower seeds, grain, plant seeds, pulses and even those that you find on a spice rack! Then all you need to do is find some thick cardboard, a piece of MDF or a picture frame and some PVA glue. You can either create a picture of an object, such as a vase of flowers, or go for a more abstract version – but make sure you don't commit to the gluing part until you are ready.

Props and Preparation: Egg boxes make ideal containers for all the seeds you collect.

Adaptation: As well as creating seed pictures, you can decorate jars, tins or boxes with seeds and then varnish them. These will then make excellent storage items for around the home.

Sweet music

There is no doubt that music works wonders. Many people with dementia will respond to music when nothing else reaches them. Scientists are trying to work out why a person with dementia can forget the names of their loved ones, yet remember all the lyrics of a song. This is likely to be because 'musical memory' is processed in the prefrontal cortex of the brain, which is one of the last brain regions to be destroyed by dementia. What is more, most people associate music with important events and a strong emotional connection, and we know that the emotions remain after the factual memory has disappeared in a person with dementia. Music can also have a calming influence on a person with late-stage dementia, as engaging them in singing, dancing or listening to music lessens agitation and provides a welcome and soothing distraction.

84 Singing

Description: Singing is very beneficial to a person with dementia – and their carers. It provides a means of communication and expression, especially since singing uses a different area of the brain from the area involved in speech. It offers an opportunity for family members to connect with each other, and the act of singing releases 'feel-good' chemicals in the brain, which eases anxiety. You can't really go wrong with singing as an activity – although you will want to choose songs that your loved one will respond to. Try popular numbers from films, shows and when your loved one was young – sea shanties, musicals and sporting songs (such as 'Swing Low Sweet Chariot'). Songs that incorporate some sort of action also work well, and are a way to add in some beneficial physical exercise.

Props and Preparation: Find out your loved one's favourite songs and keep a record of these. You may wish to invest in a karaoke player.

Adaptation: You may wish to find out if there is a local 'Singing for the Brain' group that your loved one could join. Don't forget that you can also make up your own lyrics as a family. A popular song, ready for adaptation, is 'Quartermaster's Store'. If you're not sure how this song goes, then you can look it up on the internet. As individuals progress into late-stage dementia, music from their childhood, such as folk songs, works well.

85 Listening

Description: Music can be used in many different ways to help you care for your loved one. Listening to up-tempo music can rouse your loved one, encourage movement and help motivate them to engage in daily tasks. On the other hand, sedative music (such as ballads and lullabies) can calm, quieten and help prepare for bedtime. To create a sense of comfort – as well as giving opportunities for engagement – try out classic folk songs and others with easy to remember lyrics, such as 'You are my Sunshine'.

Props and Preparation: You may find it useful to keep a record of your loved one's responses to different types of music and when they might best be used. For example, is there a particular song that stops them falling asleep at the dinner table? Experiment with different types of music, and take note of the reactions you receive.

Adaption: Listening to music can trigger all sorts of memories, feelings and emotions. Use music as a tool for reminiscence by encouraging your loved one to look at pictures whilst the music is playing. Using two different senses – listening to music and looking at pictures – is often more effective at recalling memories than one alone.

86
Dancing

Description: Dancing is an activity that relies on our 'muscle memory' – an unconscious process that the body just 'knows' how to do. It is also an important form of non-verbal communication and expression, and helps us to feel connected to each other. As well as being a fun and beneficial activity in its own right, dancing can be used to reminisce and stimulate memories of days in the dance halls.

Props and Preparation: Find out your loved one's favourite dance. Is it the foxtrot, cha-cha-cha, jive or even the bunny hop?

Adaptation: A 'circle dance', as the name suggests, involves standing or sitting in a circle, and moving as one. You can sway, follow some simple sequences or gently move around in a circle. Moving together in this way will also help everyone to feel connected as a family unit, and your loved one to feel 'safe' within the circle.

87
Quizzing

Description: There are numerous ways to design musical quizzes and challenges – and here are just a few to get you started. 'Name that tune' involves playing the first part of a song and getting everyone to guess the name and artist. 'Musical bingo' entails creating a bingo card with the names of twelve songs (or more if you wish), and the objective is to cross off the name of the song as you hear it. You could play a version of charades, but using popular songs or nursery rhymes as the theme; and how about 'Finish the lyric', where you challenge people to share the next line of a song. You can also create your own musical trivia quiz.

Props and Preparation: The activities above will require some preparation in advance, such as making a 'playlist' of the songs for the games, designing the bingo card and writing out the names of some songs on cards for the game of charades.

Adaptation: Children may well enjoy making their own 'Sing or Dare' game. They create a set of cards with various different singing challenges, such as sing 30 seconds of your favourite song, and a different set of cards with 'dares', such as hopping on one foot five times or playing air guitar for 30 seconds.

88 Conducting

Description: That's right, there is even the potential to engage your loved one in conducting music, from the comfort of the home. With the Wii Music game not only can you play the piano and bang the drums with just a wave of your hands, but you can conduct a whole orchestra by waving the remote around. The beauty of it is you can't go wrong; however erratically you use the remote, it will still sound great.

Props and Preparation: Naturally, to play this game, you will need to acquire a Wii games console and purchase a copy of the Wii Music game. This isn't a cheap activity – but with all the different games and activities available to you on the Wii, it is a good investment.

Adaptation: You can play solo or as a family 'band' using Wii Music. The wonderful thing about it is that unlike other games, which penalise players if they don't play perfectly, you can't make any 'mistakes' with Wii Music.

More arts, crafts and music activities

89 Colouring

Colouring is an activity that can leave many carers for people with dementia divided on opinion. Is this activity too childish and demeaning, or is colouring another example of a therapeutic, beneficial activity? This is really for your loved one to decide. Central to the success of any activity is incorporating an opportunity for 'choice'. No activity should be forced just because you think it is a good idea and it will occupy the time. Lay out a selection of more adult-focused colouring pictures and pens and start colouring yourself, or with your children. If your loved one wants to join in, then you know you are on to a winner. Using old-fashioned wax crayons will tug at layers of memories and the distinctive smell is likely to transport your loved one back in time.

90 Card-marking

Making your own cards is not only fun and money-saving, but a unique, personalised card means so much more than a shop-bought one. This isn't just an activity based around family birthdays and Christmas, you can make your own 'Thank You', 'Congratulations', Easter, 'Get well soon' or 'Just to say ...' cards. It's an activity with a real purpose! Your loved one may need some assistance with cutting – but make sure you offer this in a non-judgemental way. To be on the safe side, it's best to use round-tipped scissors to protect against accidental injury. You can buy card-making kits or go online to get inspiration for your own style of card-making. The possibilities are endless!

91 Recycling old cards

'Make do and mend' was a mantra the older generation lived by – and it's making a comeback! Your loved one will appreciate the thrifty nature of this activity, and the fact that it results in something useful. You can make a bookmark by cutting a strip from one of your favourite, old greetings cards, use a hole punch to make a hole at the top and then thread a piece of ribbon through the hole. How many other uses for old greeting cards can your family come up with?

92 Tracing

Whereas tracing does involve your fine motor skills in order to use the pencil to trace and the other hand to steady and move the tracing paper, it is still a therapeutic activity that all the family can enjoy. If your loved one was once a seamstress, then they will recall using tracing paper to mark their pattern's lines. By finding some old patterns, you can replicate this familiar activity, or select your own pictures to trace around.

93 Brass rubbing

If you're planning a family visit to a church, cathedral or castle, then how about doing a brass-rubbing activity whilst you are there? This activity was a popular Victorian pastime and remains so today. Many places will provide you with the specialist paper and waxes or crayons that you need.

94 Make a paper fortune teller

Paper fortune tellers have been around since the 1950s, and are an introduction to the art of origami. Having constructed your fortune teller from folding a piece of paper, you put different colours on the outside sections, numbers on the inside sections and made-up 'fortunes' on the inside tabs. For full instructions on how to make a paper fortune teller, visit www.parentsandfamilies.com.

95 Stringing beads and jewelry making

Stringing beads is a soothing, repetitive activity that engenders a sense of success for your loved one. It doesn't require any complicated thought processes or lay your loved one bare to a sense of 'failure'. Those in the early stages of dementia will be able to string small beads and follow a pattern – as long as their eyesight and dexterity allows. For people in the moderate to late stages of dementia, it is a good idea to use larger wooden beads, which can be bought for this specific purpose.

96
Make a tactile apron

This is a project for the family to undertake: making a tactile apron for your loved one. The idea behind the tactile apron – although it can just as easily be a blanket – is to provide something that occupies the hands (and therefore decreases fidgeting and agitation) of someone with dementia. Begin by coming up with a list of everything that provides tactile stimulation that could be included on the apron. You could start your list with zips, Velcro poppers, buttons, magnetic flaps, ribbons, crushed velvet and curtain tassels. Then all you need to do is securely sew these items on to your apron or blanket. Of course, you can always 'cheat' and buy a ready-made one from a specialist store that caters for people with dementia.

97
Making doilies

A doily is a decorative mat – either crocheted or made from paper (the cheaper alternative) – which can be used to protect or decorate furniture surfaces, wrap around a bouquet of flowers, decorate plates for food presentation or even as a head covering. The 1950s were the heyday of the doily, as a reaction to post-war austerity, and they became a symbol of high class. No cake stand was complete without one! Sadly, sales of doilies are now in decline – but you can do your bit as a family to bring them back in fashion! You can make your own using a square sheet of paper and scissors, or, if your loved one can crochet, you can look up various patterns on the internet. If there is a wedding in the family coming up, then paper doilies can be used in all manner of ways – from garland to favour cones or to liven up wrapping paper for a vintage look. You'll find plenty of inspiration for creative activities with doilies at www.parentsandfamilies.com.

98
Fuzzy Felt animals

Fuzzy Felt is a truly nostalgic purchase for anyone who remembers the iconic and fun activity where you stick different shapes or silhouettes of felt on to a coloured backing board. The toy was invented during World War Two, when it was discovered that children enjoyed sticking left-over bits of felt from tank components to the back of table mats! You can buy all sorts of different Fuzzy Felt themes and sets, including fairy tales, on the farm, at the hospital and a Noddy themed one. Why is this a beneficial activity for someone living with dementia? The feel of the pieces encourages tactile stimulation, and the brightly coloured felt will awaken the visual sense. It allows for creative expression without this creativity relying on an 'ability' to draw, which may be diminished in someone with dementia. It is also an activity that can be enjoyed by all the generations together, as you each contribute to a part of the Fuzzy Felt theme.

99 Make a sock monkey

Making sock monkeys is a great family activity because you can all help each other out – and delight in the sense of achievement gained from turning a pair of socks into an adorable and one-of-a-kind toy monkey. Sock monkeys also have a reminiscence value. They became popular in the 1950s when an American sock company produced a design with a red heel, which made the perfect centrepiece for a sock monkey's mouth when the socks wore out. A sock monkey pattern was, and still is, included with every pair of Rockford red heel socks. It is possible to download patterns for sock monkeys on the internet or, for a simpler alternative, you can buy do-it-yourself kits, with pre-sewn parts to avoid having to get out the sewing machine.

100 Decorating placemats

Make mealtimes more 'personal' by decorating a placemat for your loved one and other family members. Your starting-point for this activity should be to talk to the family about dementia-friendly design, using the tips under the earlier section on 'Creating a dementia-friendly home'. Remember that patterns can be confusing for someone with dementia, and you need to make it easy for them to distinguish between the plate and the placemat (so make sure you use different colours). Avoid using pictures of food because these can be confused with the real thing. You may wish to design three different placemats for breakfast, lunch and dinner to help your loved one recognise which meal of the day they are eating. The easiest way to personalise a placemat is to use a piece of thin card or paper and, when you have created your deign, put this through a laminator. It is also a good idea to round off the corners with a pair of scissors. How about also personalising a mug with a digital reproduction of a favourite old photo?

101 Bottle garden

This is a fantastic indoor project for all the family – and your loved one is likely to recall making a bottle garden in their childhood. Start by finding a suitable glass container for your garden, such as a goldfish bowl, old-fashioned sweetshop jar or a glass bottle with a cork stopper. It will help if your bottle has a wide enough opening for you to get your hands in – but this is where the younger grandchildren are useful! Start by putting some shingle, or washed pebbles, on the bottom before adding some potting compost. Choose your plants wisely; they will need to be small and the sort that thrive in humid atmospheres. You can get some ideas at www.parentsandfamilies.com. Finish by adding a final layer of grit to hold your compost in place and make your bottle garden look prettier. Your garden won't need much watering and it should be kept in a well-lit place. Please note that you may have to improvise with your 'garden tools' – using kitchen tongs and a wooden spoon to get your plants in place!

102 Build a birdhouse

You can buy all sorts of do-it-yourself kits to build specific items for around the home, where all that is required is the slotting together of the pieces. Building your own birdhouse will not only bring a shared sense of achievement, but it will attract more birds to your garden. Birdwatching is an activity many people enjoy, and listening to birdsong has been found to have a therapeutic effect. You don't have to stop at building birdhouses either. How about making bat boxes, bee boxes, beetle buckets and hedgehog homes? Find out more at www.parentsandfamilies.com.

103 Sanding wood

Like cleaning and polishing, if you plan to engage your loved one in sanding and varnishing a piece of wood, you should reinforce the fact that this isn't a time-filler; it's a practical and purposeful activity. Whereas you will still reap the tactile benefits of 'just' sanding wood – and it will evoke memories from the past – this activity will be even more successful if you identify the end goal, and link it to a gift, room decoration or some other kind of practical purpose. For example, you could sand and varnish a variety of door stops.

104 Make a playlist

There is no doubt that music can transport you back to a treasured place in time, awaken memories and generally make you feel better about the world! Nowadays, you can buy MP3 players that are very straightforward to use – and this provides the perfect opportunity to create your loved one a 'playlist' of their favourite music. You should consider a mix of both soothing and rousing music, songs to sing along to and songs that link to particular memorable occasions in their life. See www.parentsandfamilies.com for ideas on the sorts of songs you could include.

105 Old-time musicals

Watching an old-time musical film is a magical experience as you feel as though you are actually at the theatre, with the performers singing and dancing whilst looking directly at the camera. Musical films also combine two things that are very beneficial to people with dementia: singing along and accessing further back memories of watching the musicals during their past life. You'll be amazed at how your loved one will remember the lyrics and melodies. What is more, research has found that singing classic numbers from the hit musicals can boost the brain function of people with Alzheimer's disease, when compared with others who just listened. Make sure you all sing along as a family! The 1930s through to the 1960s are considered to be the golden age of the musical film – with Singin' in the Rain, The Sound of Music, Oklahoma!, The Band Wagon, Meet Me in St. Louis and The Wizard of Oz being just a few you should make sure you watch together.

106 Attend a concert

There are many different ways to bring music into your loved one's life, including attending a concert together. People with dementia connect with music in a special way – and it continues to move and motivate, even when dementia is in the advanced stages. Be careful about taking your loved one to a concert with big crowds and too much noise. People with dementia are extremely sensitive to their surroundings, and you should be aware of what triggers agitation in your loved one. Noise is a known stressor to people with dementia – and what is normally their favourite music can become upsetting if it is played too loud. For this reason, you may find that intimate recitals, or your children's school concert, are best.

Picnics

There is nothing that brings a family together quite like an old-fashioned picnic. Picnics were an extremely popular pastime – especially for families who couldn't go on long holidays, but who could sacrifice a day's work for a picnic excursion. For a person with dementia, picnics truly engage all the senses and bring memories of happy times flooding back. There is something about eating outdoors that makes flavours take on new depths, while the act of eating 'finger food' is a tactile activity, and the smell of pies baking in the oven or freshly mashed boiled eggs will transport your loved one back to the wonderful picnics of bygone years. What is more, a picnic is an excuse for an outing – and you can pick a spot away from the overwhelming hustle and bustle of crowds.

107

Picnic games

Description: There are so many different family games you can play to liven up your picnic: frisbee, croquet, badminton, skipping and relay races, like the wheelbarrow race and egg-and-spoon race. Hula-hooping was a very popular craze in the 1950s, and children, teens and adults spinning hoops around their waists and hips became an iconic 1950s image. The ring toss is another popular, old-fashioned picnic game, and you can make your own by painting some bottles in bright colours, placing these in a wooden crate and purchasing some small rubber rings.

Props and Preparation: Our website, www.parentsandfamilies. com, provides instructions on how to make your own ring-toss game. Make sure you choose games that are suited to everyone's abilities, so no-one feels left out.

Adaptation: For something more sedate, how about planning a family scavenger hunt? This is an activity that children and grandparents can do together. You can tailor this to the location for your picnic so, if you are visiting the seaside, then you will want to include items such as seashells and pebbles. Prepare some cards in advance with pictures of items you want the family to collect.

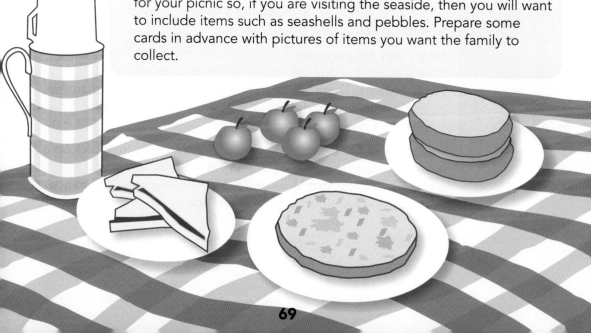

108
What a spread!

Description: Enjoy a real taste of nostalgia by preparing and packing a traditional picnic spread. The preparation for your picnic should be just as pleasurable for the whole family as the actual outing itself – and the following foods are all things you can prepare together. A memorable picnic would have included things like: devilled eggs, potato salad, cheese and pineapple, cold roast chicken, cold baked ham, a variety of sandwiches (all wrapped in waxed paper), chicken and leek pie, scotch eggs, pork pies, home-made sausage rolls, pasties, pickles and jellies, fizzy drinks in glass bottles, a thermos flask of tea and freshly squeezed lemonade.

Props and Preparation: No picnic is complete without a genuine wicker or woven picnic basket, a red-and-white gingham picnic blanket, and a wide-brimmed straw hat! You may also wish to hire a special Polaroid camera for your outing and capture and instantly share your treasured memories from the day.

Adaptation: Making freshly squeezed lemonade in preparation for a picnic will be something stored in the long-term memory of your loved one. Try and find out the method or equipment they used to use, to make the activity all the more familiar. Their sense of smell will undoubtedly be stimulated by the smell of the freshly squeezed lemons.

109
Picnic at home

Description: If packing up and heading out on an excursion is too much, or the weather takes a turn for the worse, then recreate the moment at home. You can still enjoy your traditional picnic spread and lay out the gingham picnic blanket. A picnic used to be an occasion to dress up for, so your loved one could be encouraged to put on a casual floral dress and a wide-brimmed hat (women) or a plaid shirt and khaki trousers (men).

Props and Preparation: For a home-made, as well as a home-based, picnic experience, you could have a go at making your own picnic baskets. There are instructions at www.parentsandfamilies. com. You may also wish to look online for old films featuring picnic scenes, as a basis for reminiscence.

Adaptation: For truly authentic picnic inspiration, then pick up a copy of Kenneth Grahame's *The Wind in the Willows*, and read the scene when Ratty and Mole go for a riverside picnic. You may wish to read this story aloud to your loved one.

Outside

Combining a good dose of vitamin D (through soaking up the rays outside) with a moderate amount of physical exercise can be very beneficial to someone with dementia. It can improve cardiovascular health, aid sleep, impact positively on self-esteem – and recent studies have shown that it may even improve your memory and slow down mental decline. Being outside will also stimulate memories of childhood, recalling days when your mother would simply say, 'you kids go outside and play.'

110

Daisy chains

Description: Making daisy chains is a relaxing and therapeutic activity for all the family. It's best to pick daisies with long, thick stalks, as you will need to make a slit with your fingernail about half an inch from the end of the stalk. You thread a daisy through this slit, and then continue until you have made a chain as long as you want.

Props and Preparation: The only thing you will need is a long-enough thumbnail to make a hole in the stalk and a location with lots of daisies! This activity is naturally suited to late spring or early summer when the daisies are in bloom!

Adaptation: Challenge family members to see who can make the longest daisy chain and set about making necklaces, bracelets or crowns for each other. You can also use buttercups to do the same thing. How about combining this activity with a visit to a National Trust property – to further awaken the feelings of nostalgia – and enjoy a picnic at the same time.

111

Fly a kite

Description: Nowadays you can buy all kinds of different kites – although nothing will bring memories flooding back like a red, old-fashioned diamond-shaped kite with a cross frame. Whatever type of kite you choose, many happy hours can be spent watching your kite soar in the breeze.

Props and Preparation: All you will need for this activity is a kite and the right conditions for flying it. If you wish to follow the alternative version to this activity (described below), then you will need to gather a few more materials.

Adaptation: It is not as difficult as you think to make your own kite, using newspaper, wooden dowelling (or bamboo sticks), string, tape and a strip of fabric for the tail. The shed is the perfect location for this activity! As an indoors or outdoors alternative, you can make your own mini parachute. For this, you need a plastic bag (or lightweight piece of material) cut into an octagon shape, with a small hole near the edge of each side. Cut eight pieces of string, all the same length, attach one to each of the holes and tie the string to the object you are using as a weight. Watch it fly! There are further instructions on making a kite and a mini parachute, as well as other ideas on activities with things that fly, at www.parentsandfamilies.com.

112
Conkers

Description: Conkers is a game that has been played every autumn for generations. To prepare your conker for its 'match', you should make a hole through it with a skewer and then bake it in the oven for a few hours to harden it. Then thread a piece of string, about 12 inches long, with a large knot at one end, through the conker. The game is played between two people, and they take turns hitting each other's conker using their own. The conker that eventually breaks the other person's wins a point.

Props and Preparation: For a full list of rules, see www.parentsandfamilies.com. It is tradition, on finding the first conker of the season, to say, 'Oddly oddly onker my first conker'. This is supposed to bring you competitive luck!

Adaptation: In the good old days, children made their own entertainment, using just their imagination and a bundle of energy. Here are another couple of activity ideas, requiring nothing more than some items you can forage for in the great outdoors! To play pooh-sticks, all you need is a bridge over some water and a stick for each player. Drop your sticks over the bridge at the same time, and the winner is the one whose stick emerges out the other side first. You could also set up your own snail race, utilising some twigs to make designated lanes. Line them up and wait (some time) for the winning snail to cross the finishing line.

113
Lawn games

Description: The advantage of lawn games is that they are easy to learn, and can be played whatever your age and ability. They are truly intergenerational. Croquet, in particular, is well suited to people with dementia because of the simple rules and the fact that the four balls in a croquet set are of different colours, making them easier to see and identify. As well as croquet, you can play lawn bowls, badminton, hoopla and bocce ball, to name but a few.

Props and Preparation: All you will require is a flat area of lawn and the equipment for your chosen game. Whilst vintage sets are likely to spark off additional memories, modern-day equivalents of lawn games will create just as much enjoyment.

Adaptation: Nowadays, you can also purchase adaptive versions of various different games, including chair crazy golf and a giant inflatable hoopla. These are also lawn games that can be played inside, space permitting. If you are feeling adventurous as a family, have a go at making your own coconut shy.

114 Autumn leaves

Description: You'll be amazed what you can do with autumn leaves: walk through them, rake them, collect them, identify them and make things with them! Tapping into the creativity of a person living with dementia is fundamental to their well-being, and coming up with new and different activities that combine craft and creativity with being outdoors is bound to be successful. You can collect leaves from your garden or make a special trip out to a nearby park or woodland.

Props and Preparation: There is a vast amount of inspiration on the internet: making leaf crowns, leafy collages, catching and collecting leaves, leaf rubbing and even making a candle holder from pressed leaves and découpage paste.

Adaptation: If your loved one's dementia is in the moderate to late stages, then you may wish to consider making an autumn sensory tub. This is something that all of the family can create together, capitalising on all the different colours and textures that are abundant during autumn. You could include dry and crispy leaves, fir cones, acorns and seeds.

Green fingers

Gardening is a great way to introduce physical activity into your loved one's daily routine. It is a low-impact activity, so is suitable for people of all ages and abilities, and it helps to improve muscle strength, flexibility and coordination. The sunshine and fresh air will also improve appetite and sleep, and help your loved one to feel more relaxed when they return indoors. Gardening is a truly multi-sensory activity – taking in the smell, texture and appearance of the plants and flowers, and listening to the sounds of nature. What is more, the physical motions of sweeping, raking and digging are usually movements that come quite naturally, even for a person in the mid to late stages of dementia.

115 Potting and growing

Description: Potting and growing is a creative activity, which starts from choosing the seeds you wish to plant. It is also a therapeutic activity as you watch something you have nurtured and cared for grow. You could start with growing herbs as they can be repotted as they grow, so your loved one can repeat the activity, transferring from one pot to another.

Props and Preparation: Ideally you need to find a place that receives at least five hours of sunlight a day, such as a south-facing windowsill. Before you choose which plants to pot and grow, it is best to check that they are not toxic if accidentally eaten. You can find a list of common toxic houseplants at www.parentsandfamilies.com.

Adaptation: For a true sense of accomplishment, grow plants that you can eat and use. Mint is not only easy to grow, but it can be used to make mint tea and in different recipes. There are also different varieties – from the classic old English to chocolate mint – and the scent of the plant will definitely awaken the senses. As a family, you may wish to decorate, and personalise, your own growing pots.

116 Flower arranging

Description: Flower arranging is a meaningful activity for people with dementia and provides mental and sensory stimulation, as well as an opportunity to express creativity. The sense of accomplishment when your loved one sits back and admires their creation will trigger a 'moment of joy' and a rekindling of purpose and competence – particularly when the arrangement then takes pride of place on the family table. When doing this therapeutic activity as a family, you will find that conversation will flow naturally due to the closeness of working together on the task. Use this opportunity to reminisce and talk about the flower arrangement.

Props and Preparation: Set up a table with vases of different shapes and sizes, dried or fresh flowers, and a few ribbons. If you are using fresh flowers, pick ones with sturdy stems, which can be arranged and rearranged. You could go to the flower shop together and let your loved one choose which flowers to buy.

Adaptation: As an alternative to fresh flowers, source a collection of silk flowers in all different colours, sizes and types. With such a variety, you can sort the flowers by colours and create different arrangements according to the season or theme. For example, you can create an arrangement of spring flowers or create a special Mother's Day teacup arrangement, using the small flowers and a vintage cup and saucer.

117 Weeding and raking

Description: There are many different aspects to gardening: digging, sweeping pathways, composting, watering, raking up leaves, weeding, pruning, planting, mowing the grass, trimming the edges and clearing the paths. All these different aspects are beneficial to a person with dementia because not only do they engage different muscle groups of the body and build strength and dexterity, but being outside boosts oxygen levels in people who would otherwise spend most of their time indoors. Furthermore, gardening utilises your large muscle groups (what is known as gross motor movements) and these types of activities are generally more successful for a person with dementia than those that use smaller muscle groups required for more intricate work (known as fine motor movements).

Props and Preparation: Draw up a year-round calendar of gardening activities that you can do with your loved one. You will need to bear health and safety in mind and not venture out if paths are wet and there is a risk of slipping. Make sure you have a Plan B, such as planting seeds or watering plants indoors.

Adaptation: Your loved one may enjoy gardening even more if you can acquire some old-fashioned gardening tools. Not only will these be instantly more familiar to the person with dementia, but it opens up opportunities for reminiscence. Restoring old garden tools could become a new project for the family – and another great shed-based activity. There are even local 'men in sheds' community projects, including the restoration of garden tools, which your loved one can join.

More relaxation, exercise and outside activities

118
Progressive muscle relaxation

Progressive muscle relaxation is a simple technique that helps you to become more relaxed. What is more, research has shown that it can be beneficial to people with mild to moderate dementia by decreasing agitation and helping memory recall. It works by getting you to tighten and then relax each muscle group, starting at one end of your body and working your way through. Get a taster of the technique by extending your arms in front of you, clenching your fists tightly for five seconds, and then relaxing them for ten seconds, whilst feeling the warmth and relaxation in your hands. Before doing this as a family, you should consult with your doctor if anyone has a history of muscle spasms, back problems or anything else that could be aggravated by tensing muscles.

119
Hand massage

Whereas dementia robs you of your ability to remember facts and events, you don't lose the capacity to feel human emotions or recognise a caring touch. This is why hand massage can be so beneficial and can immediately calm and reassure your loved one. It is also a different way of communicating when words begin to fail. You should always ask your loved one's permission before starting a massage and a simple way to do this is to offer to put (hypoallergenic) lotion on their hands.

120
Manicure

A manicure provides quality, one-on-one time with your loved one, away from the bustle of family life. This is something that can easily be done at home, with just a nail file and nail trimmers, a nail buffer, cuticle or hand cream and some nail polish. Given that how we feel about ourselves is closely linked to the way we look, it is important to encourage your loved one to continue to take pride in their appearance. Complimenting them on how they look will help them to feel good about themselves.

121
Hair brushing

It is not uncommon for people with dementia to become less concerned with their appearance and to lose interest in, or forget about, personal hygiene. It may be that, over time, your loved one may lose the fine motor control needed to use a hairbrush or they may even forget what a hairbrush looks like. One way around this is to turn tasks like brushing hair into a relaxing activity that you do together. You can brush each other's hair, creating an opportunity for your loved one to 'copy' the hair-brushing action that you perform.

122
Relaxing yoga

Yoga is good for the mind and body. One of the reasons why it's beneficial for people with dementia is that it requires you to focus on one pose at a time, so there is no need to over-load the brain with remembering too many things at once. Yoga can help with breathing and relaxation, meditation and stretching the body, which improves balance and flexibility and enhances mood. Make sure you seek advice from your family GP before you do anything – and this is an activity that it's advisable to do at an organised class, with a qualified instructor. However, one of the great things about yoga is that it's suitable for all ages, so you can take part as a family. There is even an adaptation called 'chair yoga', which you can do from a seated position.

123
Laughter yoga

Laughter yoga is a unique technique devised by a doctor from India in 1995, combining laughter with intentional yogic breathing. It is a good excuse to simply laugh for no reason, and since the body doesn't know the difference between real laughter and fake laughter, you can reap all the mood-enhancing health benefits. Laughter yoga is so apt for a person with dementia because there is no punchline of subtle humour to understand, so laughing doesn't depend upon the ability to process and understand the joke that has been told. There are over 6,000 laughter clubs in 60 different countries, so it won't be difficult for all the family to try out a new laughter yoga club. If you want to try this out on your own first, then visit www.parentsandfamilies.com for some simple instructions.

124 Stress balls

There are many benefits and uses to a stress ball – and making your own is a fun and meaningful activity. Squeezing a stress ball can help with dexterity and improve strength in the hands. In fact, you could even go as far as designing your own hand and finger workout! Your loved one can take comfort from squeezing the ball when they are feeling agitated or anxious and it will help to combat the problem of 'restless' hands. What is more, it can also be used for some of the ball games mentioned in this book. To make your own stress ball, all you need is some coloured balloons, a funnel and some flour. Make sure you add a second layer to your ball by stretching another balloon over the first layer. For further instructions, see www.parentsandfamilies.com.

125 Chair-based exercise

Whilst this isn't an activity you can just launch into – and it's better to seek out a qualified chair-based exercise practitioner for any proper strength-based routines – it's important for the family to consider the potential for various forms of exercise that can be done sitting down. This type of exercise lends itself well to using a variety of props, which in themselves stimulate the senses. You can use pompoms, maracas, tambourines, streamers, top hats, scarves or your home-made stress balls. Pick some music with a foot-tapping rhythm and design a routine that is repetitive and easy to follow. You could create some picture cards of some of the exercises, which you can hold up, and it will help if you face your loved one when leading the routine. Aim for about 20 minutes of activity. For some ideas, visit www.parentsandfamilies.com.

126 Yarn

The key to a successful activity for someone with moderate to late-stage dementia is to adapt an activity that they may have enjoyed previously. Whilst their knitting days may be a thing of the past, your loved one can still undertake the purposeful task of rolling up a ball of wool. This activity follows a simple, rhythmic motion, which is ideal to keep hands busy and therefore help to reduce agitation. Thicker wool will be easier to roll and the ball will 'grow' faster.

127 Pet therapy

If your loved one is an animal lover, then introducing a pet into family life can be beneficial. Owning a pet naturally introduces a range of new, meaningful and purposeful activities into daily life – walking the dog, grooming, playing, feeding and petting. People with dementia may withdraw from interacting with people but 'come alive' in the presence of a pet, since there are no concerns about being misunderstood or unable to communicate. Spending time with an animal can have a calming effect and the source of 'unconditional love' can raise the spirits of someone living with dementia. There are professional organisations that offer Animal Assisted Therapy (AAT) or, if you are considering getting your own pet, it is absolutely essential that you find one with the right temperament.

128 Fish tank

You may be surprised at the results of research into the health benefits of aquariums. Researchers have found that fish tanks can reduce levels of stress, create a calming effect, aid insomnia and even encourage people with dementia to eat more when an aquarium is placed in a dining area! The movement of brightly coloured fish can be almost hypnotic and it keeps attention focused. It is important that you consult an expert when choosing the fish to go in your tank – as although they may look visually appealing, there are certain types of fish that can't be mixed together.

129 Walking

There are a multitude of benefits to be gained from going for a walk together. Gentle exercise may improve the blood flow to the brain, help prevent muscle weakness, reduce sleep problems and improve mood. Of course, you need to factor in the impact that dementia has on your loved one's mobility and balance, as some forms of dementia can particularly affect this – and seek professional, medical advice if your loved one has any underlying medical issues. You may find that your loved one naturally wants to walk at particular times of the day – at the time when they would have walked the dog after work, for example – and this is something you can embrace. How about combining walking and reminiscence by following the path of an old railway line or retracing steps around the football field where your loved one used to play? If you are worried about your loved one getting lost when you are outside of the home environment, then there is a range of assistive technology that can help. See www.parentsandfamilies.com for more information.

130
Feed the ducks

Sometimes the simplest activities are the best. Who doesn't have a fond memory of saving up the crusts of bread, packing them into a brown paper bag and heading off to a nearby lake to feed the ducks? Your loved one will enjoy breaking up the bread – an instinctive, repetitive action, which doesn't require much thought – and benefit from the vitamin D and exercise from being outdoors.

131
Wii Fit

Did you know that several studies have found that older adults are more motivated to participate in game-based rehabilitation over conventional exercise-based rehabilitation? This might be because technologies, such as the Wii Fit, combine social interaction with exercise, and use engaging visual imagery to improve your strength, balance and fitness. You can play pretty much any game – from bowling to conducting an orchestra – all from the comfort of your own home. Bowling is a very popular game because it provides moderate exercise and it brings the atmosphere and competitiveness of a bowling alley into your living room. It is easy to organise your own family contest or tournament.

Food, glorious food

Dementia can affect a person's attitude to, and enjoyment of, food. It can therefore be beneficial to use eating as an opportunity for activity and reminiscence. For example, given how dementia affects recent memory first, your loved one may experience difficulty recognising certain foods and it may help to stimulate memory and recognition by preparing traditional dishes and favourite foods from the past. Mealtimes and food should also be an opportunity for social interaction and enjoyment.

132 Peppermint creams

Description: Peppermint creams have been popular since Victorian times and, although they can be eaten all year round, are likely to stimulate memories of Christmas, and giving them as gifts. Peppermint creams are ideal to make with children as the recipe is simple and no cooking is involved.

Props and Preparation: You need 225 g (½ lb) of icing sugar, 1 teaspoon of peppermint essence, 1 egg white, a large bowl, a pastry cutter and a pastry board. Firstly, sift the sugar into a bowl. Then beat the egg white until stiff and add the sugar. Add the peppermint essence and mix well until a stiff paste is formed. Sprinkle a board with icing sugar and roll out the paste until it is about 5 mm (¼ inch) thick. Use the pastry cutter to cut out rounds and leave them on a wire tray for twelve to twenty-four hours until firm.

Adaptation: If your loved one is on a sugar-restricted diet because of diabetes, or another medical condition, then you will obviously want to avoid this activity. Peppermint creams make an ideal traditional gift and you may also wish to decorate a gift box and line it with tissue paper, to present the special sweets.

133 Pancakes

Description: It is customary on Shrove Tuesday, or Pancake Day, to observe the tradition of cooking and eating pancakes made from ingredients that were given up during the fasting period of Lent: milk, butter and eggs. Another custom was for children to pass from house to house asking for pancakes (known as 'Lent Crocking'). If they weren't given any, broken crockery would be thrown at the door!

Props and Preparation: Pancakes can, of course, be eaten at any time of the year. Offering your loved one a choice of fillings will help to reinforce a sense of independence and control.

Adaptation: How about injecting a bit of competition into Pancake Day? See how many times you can all toss a pancake in one minute.

134 Traditional cooking

Description: This is an easy activity, which makes the most of meal times as an opportunity to talk, relax and spend quality time in each other's company. In this activity, food serves as the basis for reminiscence, and it's all about recreating meals of yesteryear. To follow the old tradition, you should serve fish on a Friday, and roast on a Sunday. Sunday leftovers were served up on a Monday and/or Tuesday as a stew or pie or cold meat dishes. In the 1950s, the majority of young children drank tea with their meals. Paying careful attention to the kinds of dishes you prepare, and when you serve them, will stimulate both appetites and conversation!

Props and Preparation: Research the traditional meals you can cook and enjoy as a family, including liver and bacon, bangers and mash, lamb or pork chops, toad-in-the-hole and rice pudding. Add to the authenticity of a traditional meal by sourcing old-fashioned crockery, tablecloths and sauce bottles. However, be mindful of the fact that patterned plates can be confusing to someone with moderate to late-stage dementia.

Adaptation: Make a 'special occasion' of eating fish and chips from newspaper. Or enjoy a traditional afternoon tea of finger-sized sandwiches, scones with butter, jam and cream, cakes and plenty of tea. You might also like to organise a Family Harvest Supper, using home-grown produce, or find out whether your local church or village is putting on a communal Harvest Supper. To complement this activity, you could have a go at making a corn dolly; instructions can be found at www.parentsandfamilies.com.

135 Old recipes and utensils

Description: There is a wealth of family history, memories and traditions contained within the pages of an old recipe book, recipe cards found at the back of the kitchen drawer and those 'secret' recipes, never written down but passed along the generations. It can be great fun to collate all these old recipes into a Family Recipe Book – and a very important way to preserve our links with our past. Nowadays, it is very easy to turn these recipes into a self-published, printed book – a keepsake for generations to come and a wonderful gift and reminiscence item for your loved one.

Props and Preparation: Spend time looking through old recipe books together and sharing stories of favourite family foods. Of course, you can test out these dishes in the kitchen to check that you have the right balance of ingredients and are using the correct cooking methods. For ideas on how to create your own printed Family Recipe Book – or a calendar featuring a family recipe for each month of the year – visit www.parentsandfamilies.com.

Adaptation: How we equip our kitchen and what we use to cook with has changed immeasurably over the decades. Take a look online together at pictures of old cooking utensils – from butter churns to flour sifters – and ask your loved one to explain what they were used for. You may also be able to hire a 'Memory Box' of authentic items from your local museum.

Shopping and remembering

Activities based around the theme of shopping work well because there are plentiful opportunities for reminiscence. Many older people can remember a time when shopping was done every day and you had no refrigerator to keep things cool, when items like butter were sold by the weight in waxed paper bags, when there were no supermarkets and when clothes items were mended and re-mended to make them last. Using this theme, you can also factor in activities, based around repetitive tasks, which rely on the muscles to 'remember' an activity that was done repetitively and enjoyably in the past. This is particularly beneficial for someone in the moderate to late stages of dementia, where mental processing and following instructions is very difficult.

136
Folding and sorting

Description: Activities that tap into 'work' and the accomplishment of tasks have a positive impact on self-esteem and feeling valued within the family unit. Many will view shopping and sorting groceries as part of their 'work routine', particularly those who were housewives. Getting dementia does not change the need to be viewed by others as 'needed' and helpful.

Props and Preparation: Make a list of all shopping-based tasks and activities, which involve an element of repetition. This might be folding clothes or napkins, putting items in storage jars or refilling items.

Adaptation: This is a very simple activity that generations can do together: organise the tins in your cupboard or the spices in your spice rack so that they are all sorted in order and facing the right way.

137
Retro sweets

Description: The sense of taste tends to be increasingly affected as dementia progresses. The taste of sweet is the first taste we develop and the last one we enjoy as we reach the end of life. This is one of the reasons why you may notice that your loved one enjoys sweets more than other foods. Reminiscing about sherbet dips, gobstoppers, fruit salads, spangles, shrimps, pear drops and Barrett's sweet cigarettes will bring the memories flooding back.

Props and Preparation: There are a number of stores that sell retro sweets for you to sample – making your reminiscence a multi-sensory experience.

Adaptation: How about turning this reminiscence activity into a tasting game? Ask your loved one to close their eyes and see if they can guess the name of the sweet from just touching them or tasting them.

138
The old high street

Description: The high street has been affected by many changes in our way of life – from rationing to the arrival of supermarkets. There is a whole wealth of history to be uncovered! Make it a family project to research your local high street. How have the buildings changed? What is the oldest shop? How does your loved one remember it in their youth? Was there a Woolworths store?

Props and Preparation: This could easily become a very 'involved' project for the family and you will need to plan visits to the local library, record office, museum and even your local history society. There is a guide on www.parentsandfamilies.com to point you in the right direction. Alternatively, you may just prefer to borrow a book from the library about the history of your town and flick through the pages together.

Adaptation: Turn a Saturday morning trip to the high street into a reminiscence activity by going through your shopping list and seeing how many of the foods and other items we buy today you could have bought in a 1950s shop.

139

Guess the advert

Description: There is a fascinating history behind brands and advertising, as you will have learnt from the Advertising Archives activity! This is a game that can be played by all the family, using adverts and brands from across the decades.

Props and Preparation: Collect a range of adverts, food packaging and logos from the 1950s to the present day. Get three pieces of cardboard and cut a square hole in the centre of each one – each hole should be larger than the previous one. Place the first piece of cardboard (with the smallest hole) over the brand, advert or food packaging and see who recognises it. If no-one can, then try the cardboard with the next size up hole, and so on. You can always decide to work in teams and keep a count of the scores.

Adaptation: You might like to look at the history of one particular brand, such as Heinz. This is a great way to really get a sense of how adverts and marketing messages have changed over the decades – from clear targeting of 'housewives' with the beans' value to the modern adverts of today, which promote the 'five-a-day' benefits.

At home

An activity doesn't have to be focused around leisure and recreation. Activities around the home will help your loved one to feel like a valued part of the household, provide a sense of normality and improve their self-esteem by showing they can still manage useful tasks. Personal care activities – such as brushing hair and applying make-up – ensure dignity, which is of paramount importance in the care of people with dementia. Both of these types of at-home activities should not be overlooked when planning meaningful and beneficial activities that you can all do together as a family.

140

Pamper days

Description: Activities that are focused on relaxation, pampering and taking pride in your appearance can easily be overlooked, but they play a very important role in maintaining dignity. It is relatively easy to organise your own at-home spa day, complete with face masks, foot spa, hand massage, nail varnish and manicure, and applying make-up.

Props and Preparation: You will need to buy in the treatments and equipment for this activity, or you could hire your own beauty therapist to come and visit for the afternoon and treat the whole family. Make sure you capture the moments on camera.

Adaptation: You can have a go at making your own beauty products, which will also provide sensory stimulation for your loved one. Make your own rose-water toner, for example. For every one firmly packed cup of rose petals, pour two cups of boiling water over the top. Cover and steep until the liquid is cool, and then strain and squeeze out the liquid from the petals. Refrigerate the rose water in a sterilized jar between use. Please note that it is a good idea to test the rosewater on your inner arm before applying it to your face.

141 Household chores

Description: There are lots of tasks, both indoors and outdoors, that can provide an opportunity for meaningful activity – such as dusting, watering plants, folding laundry and cleaning silverware. These activities can be enjoyed and can easily be adapted to a person's abilities. Remember the tasks may not be performed to perfection; it is the process, and the sense of achievement, that is important. Add in a sprinkle of reminiscence by replicating the structure and routine that household chores used to take. For example, washing day would have been on a Monday, ironing on a Tuesday, shopping on a Wednesday, mending on a Thursday, and baking for the weekend on a Friday.

Props and Preparation: Draw up a list of all the household chores that your loved one can help out with. Be prepared to get them started by doing the activity with them, but resist the temptation to take over. The idea is for your loved one to do the activities themselves.

Adaptation: Use activities that are rhythmical and repetitive if your loved one struggles with multi-step tasks. Repeating a task in the same way over time creates a physical 'memory' of how to complete that task. Our muscles often remember what the mind can't.

142 Room decorations

Description: Make it a family project to really personalise the space where your loved one spends their time. Room decorations can help to reinforce personality and identity, and provide 'conversation starters' for people that come to visit. There are plenty of things you can do that will be really beneficial to your loved one. You can make, and display, a collage of old photographs, put up old pictures that trigger memories of past hobbies and interests and find large print photographs of local scenes from yesteryear. You can make the most of natural light by hanging bright objects in the window, and make stained glass trinkets that catch the sunlight. You can source old-fashioned everyday items, such as a telephone that uses a dial instead of buttons. You can even seek out products, such as Pears soap, that your loved one will recognise and remember the distinctive smell from when they were younger.

Props and Preparation: Begin by looking through old photographs together and see what really catches their attention and sparks off memories. There is no use buying a telephone from the 1970s, if a model from the 1950s triggers more recognition. The current resurgence of interest in vintage and recycling means that it is not difficult to buy reproduction items, as well as originals.

Adaptation: You can really go to town on this family project by 'retro-decorating'. This means using objects, design and colour from a time in the past that your loved one remembers.
You can find inspiration for 'retro-decorating' ideas at www.parentsandfamilies.com.

The power of smell

A simple, everyday smell can bring the memories flooding back like nothing else. As a child (and also as an adult), when you smell something for the first time, your brain immediately makes an 'emotional connection' to the associated event, person, moment or object. When you come across that smell again, the brain immediately remembers the emotional connection and you naturally recall the particular memory linked with the smell. That is why the smell of chlorine can immediately transport you back to a pool-related memory and conjure up happy thoughts of childhood. Research studies have also found out that smells have the tendency to take you further back in time than verbal or visual memory clues. This is particularly valuable for someone with dementia who is more likely to recall events from the distant past than more recent memories.

143

Baking cookies and smelling coffee

Description: Although your loved one may not be able to bake on their own, this is a great family activity for you to do together. There are many different steps in baking cookies – stirring, kneading the cookie dough, using the cookie cutters and tasting the mix – and you can share out the tasks between you. There is nothing like filling the house with the smell of freshly baked cookies to stimulate the senses, bring back memories and remind your loved one of the time when they made everything from scratch.

Props and Preparation: Due to the fact that there are a few potential hazards involved in cooking – such as using ovens and touching hot baking trays – it is important to take your loved one's degree of memory loss into consideration when planning this activity. There are lots of different recipes for cookies available on the internet – of varying degrees of difficulty.

Adaptation: How about making some freshly ground coffee to enjoy with your cookies? Your loved one will enjoy the purposeful task of grinding down the coffee beans – particularly if you are able to find an old-fashioned coffee grinder like the one they used to use.

144 Can you smell what it is?

Description: This is a smelling and guessing game you can make and play as a family. Begin by collecting a range of jars and wrap them with paper, so you can't see inside. Fill each jar with a different scent or texture – such as vanilla pods, freshly cut grass, pennies, cinnamon, lavender and mint. Pass the jars around to smell or shake, in order to guess what's inside. You could adapt this game by then asking everyone to share a memory or story associated with the smell.

Props and Preparation: All you need for this activity is a collection of jars and various items to fill them. If you can, try and use smells associated with childhood memories.

Adaptation: If making this game is too much, then you can buy a ready-made game called Le Loto des Odeurs, which includes 30 different scents for you to match up.

145 A whiff of the past

Description: This activity involves planning reminiscence activities and outings around evocative smells from the past. Given the power of smell to conjure up memories, it can be surprisingly successful to use our sense of smell as a source of inspiration. For example, oiling a cricket bat using linseed oil, enjoying fish and chips wrapped in newspaper along the seafront, watching the grandchildren swim whilst taking in the smell of chlorine at a swimming pool, or visiting a cobblers shop.

Props and Preparation: Brainstorm a list of all the smells that you can base family activities around. These might include freshly baked bread, new-mown grass, walking after the rain, lavender plants, the smell of tomato plants in greenhouses, candy floss at a fair or dusting using a particular household product from the past.

Adaptation: Ask your loved one which smells particularly remind them of their childhood and spend time reminiscing about these smells and the memories associated with them.

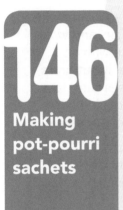

146 Making pot-pourri sachets

Description: You can make your own pot-pourri sachets or lavender bags using odd scraps of fabric, a needle and thread and a ribbon. Fold your fabric in half and cut out the shape you want your bag to be, being careful to avoid cutting the fold. You then have to sew the two pieces of fabric together, along the sides, leaving it open along the top. Turn your bag inside out and fill it with pot-pourri or lavender – and then either use a ribbon to tie the bag shut or sew it up.

Props and Preparation: All you need for this activity is some material, a needle and thread, some ribbon and some dried pot-pourri or lavender.

Adaptation: Sewing requires a degree of fine motor skills and intricate work. If this is too much for your loved one, then you can buy some ready-made organza bags or velvet pouches and fill these with lavender or pot-pourri.

More home, food and shopping activities

147 Make real orange juice

There is nothing quite like drinking your own freshly squeezed orange juice – the satisfaction and sense of accomplishment from drinking the fruits of your labour. Making orange juice using an old-fashioned orange juicer will help to develop muscle strength in the hands, and feeling the texture of the rind, smelling and tasting the juice will create a truly sensory experience for everyone involved.

148 Afternoon tea

The concept of 'afternoon tea' evolved in Britain in the early 1840s, as a way of staving off the hunger between breakfast time and the evening meal at 8pm. There was no such thing as a midday meal in those days. The traditional afternoon tea is served between 3pm and 5pm and consists of sandwiches (cut into fingers), cakes, scones and, of course, a cup of tea. To properly recreate an afternoon tea experience for your loved one, serve the tea from ornate silver teapots into bone china cups, and present your scones and cakes on a tiered cake stand.

149 Chocolate tasting

As dementia progresses, you may well find that your loved one favours sweet tastes. You can capitalise on this by organising your own chocolate-tasting family activity. Chocolate tasting is different from simply eating chocolates because you should encourage conversations between you about the smell, texture, look and, of course, taste, of the chocolate. You should limit the number of chocolates you taste to six or seven. Invite all family members to either write down what they guess the flavour of chocolate to be, or prepare some labels in advance to match up with each chocolate tasted. Of course, this isn't an activity that should be recreated on a very regular basis as sugar isn't a healthy food! For some sweet tasting alternatives, see www.parentsandfamilies.com.

150 Make a gingerbread house

With the availability of gingerbread house kits on the market, this is a fun and simple intergenerational activity. You will also find that this activity epitomises the meaning of teamwork, and you can stand back and watch the generations working together to complete the different elements of the gingerbread house. For example, your loved one could decide on where the sweet decorations should go, whilst someone else lays down the icing 'glue' to stick them down. Bear in mind that too much choice can be overwhelming for someone with dementia so you may want to limit the number of sweet choices. If you're feeling really adventurous as a family then you could set about creating your own gingerbread village!

151 Nut cracker

Cracking nuts is likely to evoke fond memories and the sound of the cracking nuts will provide a sense of comfort and familiarity. This is a simple, repetitive activity, which means that your loved one will soon become absorbed. Perhaps you can get hold of an old-fashioned nut cracker or, if your loved one struggles with their grip, choose one that is easily operated.

152 Shoe shining

In the past, shoes would have been lined up on a Sunday night and painstakingly polished by the boys of the house until you could see your reflection in them! This activity is not only likely to stimulate memories, but it makes the most of your loved one's remaining skills and abilities. To do this properly, you need to rub the shoes down with a horsehair brush, to remove any dirt, before applying the shoe polish in a circular motion. Remove any excess polish with the horsehair shoeshine brush before buffing them with a cloth or chamois. Your loved one is likely to tell you an even better way to get the perfect shine! How about going a step further and making your own traditional shoe shine box together. You can find instructions at www.parentsandfamilies.com.

153
Silver cleaning

Cleaning and polishing silverware is an activity that provides a sense of purpose through its usefulness. You should set out everything you need on a tray – silver items, polish, cleaning cloths (or squares of cotton) and cotton buds to clean the small spaces. As an alternative to using silver polish, how about cleaning silver the traditional way, using two parts baking soda to one part salt? You can even clean silver using white toothpaste (not the gel variety). As you polish, use the opportunity to reminisce about other old-fashioned home cleaning remedies.

154
Old hub caps and polish

If your loved one has an interest in motor vehicles, then polishing old hub caps together can be a therapeutic and useful activity. Whereas some hubcaps from the 1940s, '50s and '60s should only be restored by a specialist, many can be brought back to life with some metal polish (non-toxic), some scratch remover and a few other tools. This activity can be combined with reminiscing about the cars owned over the years.

155
Car wash

In coming up with a variety of meaningful activities for your loved one and your family, it is all about being resourceful. Washing the car can be turned into a leisurely Sunday afternoon activity for the family – and you can even link this to some reminiscence work about old, favourite forms of transport. There are no complicated instructions to follow and it enables your loved one to focus on one specific task in hand, such as cleaning the wheels or polishing the bodywork.

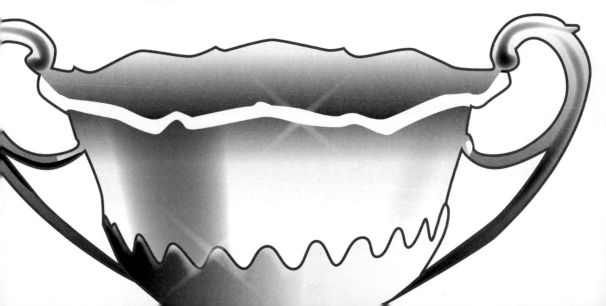

156 Helping others

When we give other people a helping hand, we feel good about ourselves. In fact, we get what researchers call a 'helper's high', a euphoric feeling that releases feel-good chemicals into our body and improves our sense of self-worth. This doesn't change because you have a diagnosis of dementia – and as a family, it can be rewarding to seek out ways to help your loved one retain their feelings of self-worth. Make a list of all the different ways you can involve your loved one, along with members of the family, in helping others. You could collect tins from neighbours to donate to the local soup kitchen, offer to help local organisations with stuffing envelopes, or help with the clean-up of the local beach.

157 Fundraising

You may well find that members of your family are inspired to want to help people affected by dementia in their local community and beyond. It can be a cathartic experience to join other families in taking part in organised fundraising activities, such as Memory Walks, and this is also an opportunity to share your personal experiences with other families living with dementia. Alternatively, you can plan your own family fundraising. How about a cake sale, a sponsored hop, a garden fête or a silent auction?

158 Therapeutic writing

Undoubtedly, there will be times when you feel things getting on top of you – and this is also likely to be the case for other family members. Writing about feelings, both positive and negative, can be very therapeutic. Keeping a diary can help children to understand their feelings, rather than bottling them up or venting them in some other way, such as by getting angry. If they want to, they can then be encouraged to share what they have written with an adult carer. You could start the ball rolling by going shopping for a diary or notebook together. Be sure to remind them that keeping a diary isn't like writing in school and encourage them to draw or doodle, instead of writing, if that's what helps.

159 Scrapbook of things you have done together

Wonderful memories to treasure forever will be made from doing the activities in this book. There will be magical moments that you will want to hold on to, and as time marches on, you may forget the important little details. Keeping a scrapbook of things you have done with your loved one will help you to preserve these special memories. All the family will get an emotional boost from looking back through the scrapbook, seeing the photos and reading the comments and observations about the impact of the activities on your loved one and the whole family. You could even create your own blog – an online scrapbook of recorded memories and moments; other families around the world will benefit from reading about, and learning from, your family's experience of living well with dementia. You can find tips on writing a blog at www.parentsandfamilies.com.

160 Feature on our website

There is no-one more able to come up with meaningful and beneficial activities for people with dementia than you. That is because you know your loved one, their interests, what makes their eyes light up and what it is like for them to live with dementia. There are hundreds of activity ideas in this book (particularly if you take into account all the different adaptations), but we know there are many more we haven't thought of. And now it's over to you. If you have an activity idea you would like to share with other families living with dementia, please log on to our website, www.parentsandfamilies.com, where you will find instructions for adding your own activities.

How to design your own activities

Here is a framework to guide you through the process of designing your own, unique dementia-friendly activities:

1. **Start here: what makes your loved one who they are?** A successful activity is built around your loved one's interests, former occupations, hobbies and passions. For example, if your loved one used to spend their time tinkering and fixing things, then consider activities based around simple construction projects, sorting nuts and bolts or building a train set or Scalextric. Make a list of 'themes' that would appeal to your loved one.

2. **Match activity to ability.** How does dementia affect your loved one's ability to 'do'? The last thing you want is for your loved one to be left with a sense of failure because they have been unable to do what you had planned. On the other hand, neither do you want the activities to be

deemed as 'childish' because they are so simple. In the early stages of dementia, your loved one will be able to follow rules and instructions, but as dementia progresses, activities should be focused on those that rely on 'muscle memory', stimulate the senses, and enable communication and expression through creative activity. In the moderate to late stages, factor in sensory stimulation (such as hand massage), repetitive activities that don't rely on intricate hand-eye coordination, and more passive activities, such as responding to music and fiddling with tactile aprons.

3. **Think about the focus and purpose.** It helps to be clear about the end-result of your activity, or what you want the 'outcome' to be. This will ensure that your activity is both purposeful and beneficial to your loved one. Your chosen outcome might be to make something, to help around the home, to play a game as a family, to stimulate specific memories or to achieve a relaxed state.

4. **Source some inspiration.** There are plenty of places you can go to trigger ideas for activities. There is a plethora of craft websites, which, with a little bit of adaptation and imagination, can be turned into dementia-friendly activities. You can take an existing activity that your loved one will have enjoyed in the past, and add a creative twist to it. For example, how many different ways can you play the game of bingo: music bingo, picture bingo or 'reminiscence bingo' (crossing off the words linked to the names of old television shows from the 1950s). How about using the activities in this book as a basis and personalising them to suit your loved one? For a real injection of creativity, try out the 'Mind Tiles' technique. This works by creating a 'new' idea by combining two other concepts. For example, what might you be able to create if you combine egg shells and mosaics? An Easter mosaic made out of painted broken egg shells rather than broken glass, tiles or pottery!

5. **Add in the successful ingredients.** There are a number of fail-safe 'ingredients' you can add to your activity:

- Social interaction: Interact with other people, develop closer bonds through shared activity, have fun and create opportunities for your loved one's stories to be heard and personality to shine through.

- Music: Even when other abilities are severely affected by dementia, people will still respond to music, rhythm and dance.

- Reminiscence: Given that dementia tends to affect our more recent memories first, activities that are associated with the more distant past are likely to be successful. Your loved one will relish the opportunity to reminisce about their days growing up.

- Tactile stimulation: When verbal communication is failing, sensory stimulation through touch, taste, hearing and smell can be a way to interpret and react to the world around us. Make sure that your activities appeal to as many of the different senses as possible.

- Sense of achievement: Succeeding at activities will help to reinforce your loved one's feelings of self-worth, usefulness and belonging as a part of the family unit.

- Intergenerational: Above all else, make your activities intergenerational. This is what this book is all about – enabling grandparents to be grandparents, regardless of their diagnosis, and grandchildren to continue to enjoy 'quality time' with their loved one, learning from them, enjoying activities together and creating treasured memories to last a lifetime.

6. **Bring in the props.** Using props, objects and equipment can really bring an activity to life. In particular, consider the ways in which you can source 'authentic', old-fashioned items from the past, which will stimulate memories and transport people back to a place in time they remember with fondness.

7. **Find a way of explaining.** How you explain an activity, initiate it or incorporate it into daily routine can make or break the success of your activity. It's just as important to spend time considering how you will motivate your loved one to participate as it is to spend time thinking creatively about what you can do.

8. **Who, where, when, how?** There are many practicalities that need to be considered. Who is going to be involved with your activity? Where will the activity take place? When is the best time of day? How long will it last?

9. **Ready, Go, Steady!** If you have thought everything through, then you are ready to go for it! However, go steady, and don't be afraid to stop the activity, or change course, if you feel it isn't working. Despite all your best intentions, there will be some activities that, for whatever reason, don't hit the spot. These activities are to be learned from, and you may find that on a different day, or at a different time, or by trying a new tack to initiative the activity, it works perfectly well.

10. **Be present.** Remember that your loved one will benefit from the positive emotional memories of enjoying an activity together, even if the details of the activities are forgotten. Your loved one will pick up on – and mirror – your own emotional engagement with the activities, so it is important that everyone involved is 'present' in the moment. Don't lose sight of why you are doing these activities and the difference you can make to the care and well-being of your loved one.

1,2,3 ... Go!

You have reached the end of the book – and you should now be ready to put everything you have learnt into practice. Before you put the book down and pick up the bagatelle, here are three more important points to finish with.

1. You will find it useful to go back through the Activities section and annotate all those that you want to try out. Keep a record of the impact each activity has on your loved one, by filling out this simple record sheet, which you can download from www.parentsandfamilies.com.

Name of activity	Adaptation	Rating	Notes
Name or number of activity as it appears in the book. Add your own activities in here too.	Is there anything you have changed with the activity, which works better for your loved one?	☺ 😐 ☹ This is for your child(ren) to score. How would they rate the activity?	A blank space for anything else you wish to add, such as the time of day best suited to this activity, and the date you first tried the activity out.

2. You need to start building up a collection of reminiscence props. From now on, you should always be on the look-out for objects and items that will trigger memories whenever you visit a car boot sale or charity shop. You can also search the internet for items, and ask other family members to see what they have squirrelled away in the loft.

3. Impress upon members of your family the importance of creating a toy time capsule, to be unveiled at some point in the future. Think about who you would like to open your capsule. Is this something for your own grandchildren or for you to open yourself in order to get a rush of nostalgia? With the number of people with dementia steadily increasing, we all need to start finding ways to keep the past alive now.